Historical Association Studies

Decolonization

Historical Association Studies

General Editors: Muriel Chamberlain, H. T. Dickinson and Joe Smith

The Historical Association, founded in 1906, brings together people who share an interest in, and love for, the past. It aims to further the study and teaching of history at all levels: teacher and student, amateur and professional. This is one of over 100 publications available at preferential rates to members. Membership also includes journals at generous discounts and gives access to courses, conferences, tours and regional and local activities. Full details are available from The Secretary, The Historical Association, 59a Kennington Park Road, London SE11 4JH, telephone: 0171-735 3901.

Decolonization: The Fall of the European Empires

Second Edition

M. E. Chamberlain

The right of Muriel Chamberlain to be identified as author of this work has been asserted in accordance with the Copyright, Designs and Patents Act 1988.

First published 1985
Reprinted 1987, 1989
Reprinted with updated further reading 1994
Reprinted 1995, 1996
Second edition published 1999

2 4 6 8 10 9 7 5 3 1

Blackwell Publishers Ltd
108 Cowley Road
Oxford OX4 1JF
UK

Blackwell Publishers Inc.
350 Main Street
Malden, MA 02148
USA

British Library Cataloguing in Publication Data

A CIP catalogue record for this book is available from the British Library.

Library of Congress Cataloging-in-Publication Data is available for this book.

ISBN 0–631–21602–2 (pbk); 0–631–21804–1 (hbk)

Typeset in 11 on 13 pt Ehrhardt by Ace Filmsetting Ltd, Frome, Somerset
Printed in Great Britain by MPG Books Ltd, Bodmin, Cornwall

This book is printed on acid-free paper

Contents

Outline Chronology

1783	Britain loses the Thirteen Colonies in North America.
1820s	Spain and Portugal lose their empires in South and Central America.
1830	France becomes involved in Algeria.
1857	Indian 'Mutiny'.
1858	East India Company cedes its remaining administrative powers in India to the British Crown.
1869	Opening of the Suez Canal.
c.1884–91	Whole continent of Africa is partitioned among the European Powers.
1885	Indian National Congress founded.
1906	Muslim League is formed.
1914	Outbreak of First World War.
1917	Montagu Declaration. The Secretary of State for India promises eventual self-government for India.
	Balfour Declaration. British Foreign Secretary declares in favour of a 'national home' for the Jews in Palestine so long as it does not prejudice the existing rights of non-Jews.
	Russian revolution.
1919	Mandate System is established by Article 22 of the Covenant of the League of Nations.
	Amritsar massacre.
1923	Union of Soviet Socialist Republics formed.
	Southern Rhodesia becomes a 'self-governing colony'.
	The Devonshire White Paper declares that Kenya is 'primarily an African territory'.
1926	Balfour Report provides classic definition of relations within the British empire and especially the meaning of dominion status.
1930	Mahatma Gandhi leads symbolic march to Dandi to pick up sea salt, thus evading the excise duty.
1931	Statute of Westminster.
1930–2	Round Table Conferences to discuss Indian affairs.

1935	Italians invade Abyssinia (Ethiopia)
	Government of India Act.
1937	Indian elections. Congress wins 8 of the 11 provinces and refuses to co-operate with the Muslim League.
	Irgun begin terrorist campaign against Arabs in Palestine.
1939	Outbreak of Second World War.
1940	Fall of France.
	Negro Governor of Chad, Felix Eboue, rejects Vichy and declares for General de Gaulle and the Free French.
1941	Japan enters war.
	British forces restore Ethiopian independence.
	Japanese occupy Indochina.
	Ho Chi Minh founds Vietminh to work for Vietnam independence.
1942	Fall of Singapore.
	Cripps offer to Indian nationalists. 'Quit India' resolution.
1945	Ho Chi Minh proclaims provisional government in Hanoi. France, despite British and American misgivings, insists on resuming control of Indochina.
1946	United Nations Trusteeship Council takes over functions of League of Nations Mandate Commission. South Africa refuses to recognize its jurisdiction in Namibia.
	'French Union' is established as part of constitution of the Fourth Republic.
	Americans back large-scale Jewish immigration into Palestine.
	Cabinet Mission tries to bridge the gap between Congress and the Muslim League to agree on terms for Indian independence. Fails.
1947	Partition of India. India and Pakistan become independent as two separate states.
	Britain refers Palestine question to the United Nations.
1948	Britain surrenders Palestine Mandate and withdraws troops. First Arab–Israeli war.
	Gandhi is assassinated by a Hindu fanatic.
	Burma becomes independent and (unusually for an ex-British colony) opts not to join the Commonwealth.
1949	Eire becomes a republic and leaves the Commonwealth.
	The Dutch withdraw from Indonesia. Sukarno becomes President.
	Formula is found by which republics can stay in the Commonwealth.
1950	India and Pakistan become republics but stay in the Commonwealth.
1953	Death of Stalin. German workers rise but are easily suppressed.
	Central African Federation is formed between Northern and Southern Rhodesia and Nyasaland.
1954	Anglo-Egyptian Agreement that Britain would withdraw all forces

1975	Indonesia seizes East Timor.
	Angola becomes independent but civil war continues.
	Mozambique becomes independent.
1979	Rhodesia negotiates settlement with London under which it temporarily returns to colonial status.
	Russia invades Afghanistan.
1980	Following elections, Rhodesia becomes independent as Zimbabwe.
	'Solidarity' becomes powerful force in Poland.
1981	Martial Law imposed in Poland.
1985	Gorbachev comes to power.
1988	Soviet troops begin withdrawal from Afghanistan.
	Unrest begins in Baltic States, Armenia, Azerbaijan, Georgia and other parts of the Soviet Union.
1989	Free elections in Poland. Victory for Solidarity.
	Berlin Wall comes down.
1990	Elections in Hungary and Czechoslovakia.
1991	Soviet Union recognizes independence of the Baltic States. Other Soviet republics, including even Ukraine and Belorussia, proclaim their independence.
	Supreme Soviet dissolves Union of Soviet Socialist Republics. (Is replaced by weak organization, the Confederation of Independent States.) Gorbachev resigns as Soviet President. Russian Federation, with Boris Yeltsin as President, takes the Soviet Union's place on the United Nations Security Council.
1994	South Africa returns to the Commonwealth, after repudiating apartheid and holding free elections.

Maps

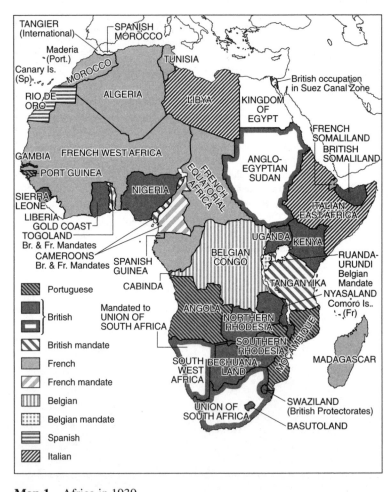

Map 1   Africa in 1939.
Source: J. D. Fage, *An Atlas of African History*, Edward Arnold, 1978, p. 48.

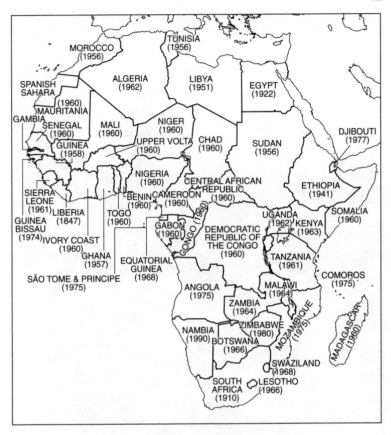

Map 2 Africa in 1998, showing independence dates.
Source: based on P. Gifford and W. R. Louis (eds), *The Transfer of Power in Africa*, Yale University Press, 1982.

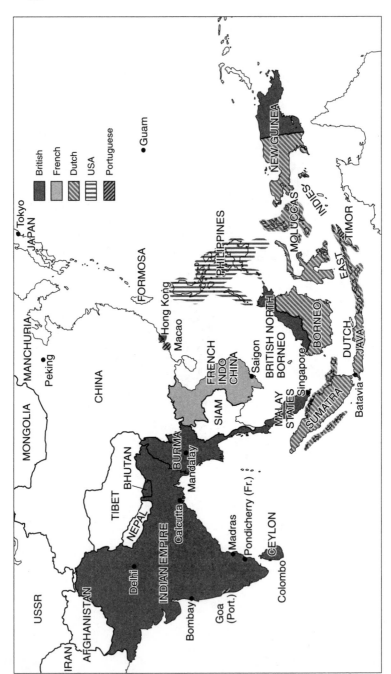

Map 3 Asia in 1939.
Source: based on *The Hamlyn Historical Atlas*, 1981, map 86.

Map 4 Asia in 1980, showing independence dates.
Source: as for map 3.

Map 5 The Soviet Empire in 1953.
Source: M. Gilbert, *Russian History Atlas*, Weidenfeld & Nicolson, 1972.

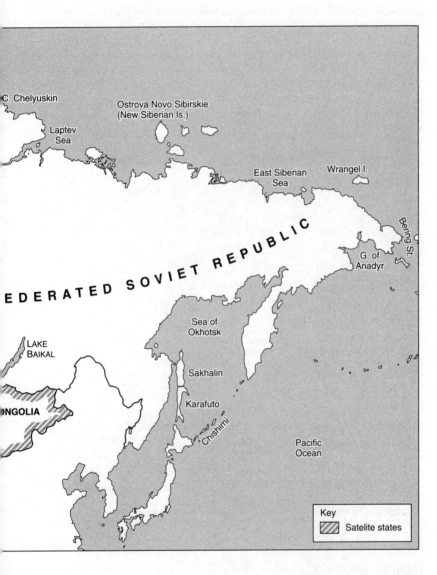

C. Chelyuskin

Ostrova Novo Sibirskie
(New Siberian Is.)

Laptev
Sea

East Siberian
Sea

Wrangel I.

EDERATED SOVIET REPUBLIC

Bering St.

G. of
Anadyr

LAKE
BAIKAL

Sea of
Okhotsk

Sakhalin

NGOLIA

Karafuto

Chishimi

Pacific
Ocean

Key

Satelite states

Chamberlain: Decolonization
Map 5

Map 6 The successor states of the Soviet Union.
Source: *The Times Concise Atlas of World History*, 1994, p. 151.

Introduction

When V. I. Lenin wrote the preface to a new edition of his *Imperialism; The Highest Stage of Capitalism*, dated from Petrograd in April 1917, he complained that, previously, Tsarist censorship had compelled him to use coded language and to pretend to be speaking of Japan and Korea. Now 'the careful reader will easily substitute Russia for Japan, and Finland, Poland, Courland, the Ukraine, Khiva, Bokhara, Estonia or other regions peopled by non-Great Russians, for Korea' (pp. 6–7). Lenin had no doubt that Russia's landward expansion over the territories of non-Russians did not differ from the overseas conquests of the maritime Powers of western Europe. On this, his interpretation seems to be vindicated by the fact that since 1988 the Soviet empire has collapsed in much the same way as the western empires. It is therefore logical to include the dissolution of the Russian empire in a book on European decolonization.

The United States provides a more difficult case. In the middle of the nineteenth century the American people generally did not doubt that it was their 'manifest destiny' to conquer the whole of the North American continent, including Canada and part of what was then Mexico. At the end of the century in what some historians regard as a 'great aberration' (S. F. Bemis, 1955, p. 463) and others as a logical development (R. W. Van Alstyne, 1960; 1974; A. E. Campbell, 1960), the United States also acquired overseas territories, Hawaii, the Philippines, Cuba and Puerto Rico. Some of these, the Philippines and Cuba, have been decolonized more or less on the European model. Others, Hawaii and Puerto Rico, have been drawn into a closer relationship with the United States. The United States is itself a 'successor state' of three European empires, the British, Spanish and French. Although it does not fit into the pattern of twentieth-century decolonization so neatly as Russia does, some consideration of American policy is also likely to be instructive.

'Decolonization' is a recent word. It only came into general use in the 1950s and 1960s, although it seems to have been coined in 1932 by a German scholar, Moritz Julius Bonn, for his section on 'Imperialism' in the *Encyclopaedia of the Social Sciences* (Seligman, 1932). Nowadays it is commonly understood to mean the process by which the peoples of the Third World gained their independence from their colonial rulers. But it has not altogether found favour with Asians and Africans because it can be taken to imply that the initiatives for decolonization, as for colonization, were taken by the metropolitan powers. Consequently, Asians and Africans have sometimes preferred to speak of their 'liberation struggles' or even their 'resumption of independence' (Hargreaves, 1979, pp. 3–8; Gifford and Louis, 1982, pp. 515, 569).

There is force in this objection, but it remains true that vital decisions were taken in London or Paris, Brussels or The Hague. Historians must try to hold the balance by examining both the policies of the colonial powers and the ideas and initiatives which came from the colonized. Both were frequently influenced by earlier historical experience. It is, therefore, also important that the historian should view the problem in a longer perspective. Decolonization took place almost entirely after the Second World War, mainly between 1947 and 1965, but it had much deeper roots than that. Some have held that the European empires had the seeds of decay within them from the beginning (Kennedy, 1984, pp. 201–3). Even if this seems too deterministic a view, it is true that both the speed and the fashion in which the various European empires were dismantled owed a great deal to earlier historical experiences and to the lessons which had been drawn, correctly or incorrectly, from them.

This is particularly so when the connection had been a long one and of great importance to both parties, as in the case of Britain and India. India must be a key case history in any study of decolonization. The story begins long before 1947. It was the largest single country decolonized, as well as the first important example of decolonization after 1945. How far India provided the model for Africa is now the subject of some scholarly debate (see pp. 10–11), but it seems beyond dispute that India was the great exemplar to which colonial nationalists in other countries looked and that the relinquishment of India in 1947 set the British empire (by far the largest of the European colonial empires) inexorably upon the path to dissolution. Where Britain led the others followed. It took a generation for all the implications to be realized, but in the end most former colonial peoples found that they were pushing at an open door. The Europeans had abandoned their attempt to dominate the rest of the world politically, although perhaps not economically. The era which had begun soon after the Renaissance had finally come to an end.

The Background

Modern Europe's first great loss of empire occurred not in the twentieth century, but in the late eighteenth and early nineteenth centuries and involved not alien peoples, temporarily under European rule, but peoples of predominantly European stock, who broke away from the colonial power to found their own nation states. Although the twentieth-century movement was sometimes concerned with the recovery of already well-defined national identities, it more often involved the creation of new nation states from hitherto diverse groups of peoples. The historic precedents of the eighteenth and nineteenth centuries cannot be ignored. They were sometimes known to, and used by, colonial peoples in the twentieth century; for example, educated Indians were aware of the American embargo on the import of British goods, which preceded the American war of independence, and created their own form of it in the *swadeshi* movement of the early twentieth century, when Indians were encouraged to boycott European goods in favour of Indian.

The collapse of these earlier empires was powerful in determining the attitudes of the colonial powers. Britain lost the bulk of her North American empire in 1776–83 when the United States was formed. The loss may not have been so shattering to Britain, either materially or psychologically, as was once supposed. Professor Harlow argued forcefully that the loss only confirmed the 'Swing to the East', which was already discernible in British policies; that is to say, a preference for trade in Asia to the expense and commitment involved in governing colonies of settlement in the western hemisphere (Harlow, 1952, pp. 1–11). Nevertheless, the American war of independence left a permanent mark on British thinking about empire. The British fairly soon reconciled themselves to the loss by arguing that it was 'natural'. Colonies were like children who would eventually grow to manhood and would then inevitably seek their independence from the mother country. Britain put no serious obstacles in the way of such growth on the part of her other colonies of settlement, Canada, Australia, New Zealand or (since in the early twentieth century it was regarded simply as another colony of white settlement like the others) South Africa. Whether the same arguments held good for non-European dependencies, like India or Britain's many tropical colonies in Africa and elsewhere, was thought to be debatable.

Britain's loss of her American colonies had not been occasioned by any collapse on the part of the metropolitan power. On the contrary, Britain was still confident in the memory of her success in the Seven Years War of 1756–63, which had given her French Canada and left her as the dominant European power in India. At home the vast economic changes, which were to make Britain for a time the leading industrial power in the world, were already under way. The loss must be traced to political mistakes in Britain, the determination of the Americans, and the international support given to the Americans by France and Spain.

The story of the collapse of the Spanish and Portuguese empires in South and Central America in the early nineteenth century is different. Both Spain and Portugal were so weakened by the Napoleonic wars that they could no longer control their American empires. Although there was fighting in some places, generally the successor states established themselves to fill a vacuum. They were often unstable and prone to lurch from one extreme form of government to another. Some historians have even speculated that a serious struggle to obtain independence is a necessary stage in the creation of a stable and disciplined state.

In the nineteenth century Spain and Portugal sank to the rank of third-rate powers. It was easy for colonial propagandists to adopt 'cause-and-effect' arguments, either in the form that the loss of colonies would inevitably lead to the loss of great power status, or that the loss of great power status would inevitably lead to the loss of colonies. Either way the possession of an empire came to be regarded as a kind of badge of great power status, important for prestige, irrespective of whether it was also worth while economically.

The great Scottish economist, Adam Smith, saw this paradox as early as 1776. He argued forcefully that, although colonies could not be other than a liability to the colonial power, no country would voluntarily relinquish them, partly because of the pressure of particular vested interests within the metropolitan country but also because of general considerations of prestige. Adam Smith's arguments help to explain why, although fashionable doctrine held during the early and mid-nineteenth centry that colonies were an economic drain and an international liability, no colonial power seriously tried to get rid of them. Britain indeed considerably expanded her empire (Robinson and Gallagher, 1953, pp. 1–15).

The late nineteenth century saw renewed competition for empire. Scholarly opinion is turning against monocausal explanations for that phenomenon. A complex mixture of economic, diplomatic, political and strategic motives led the old colonial powers like Britain, France, Holland, Portugal and Spain, joined by new colonial powers, like Germany and Italy, to reassert themselves both in the race for new colonies and in the defence of old ones.

At that time nothing was further from the mind of most governments than 'decolonization'. The future seemed to lie with the big states, such as the United States of America, or the now united German Reich. If countries like Britain and France were to remain in contention, they must do so as the centres of great empires. This, however, left room for considerable diversity in the actual organization of those empires. The French always tended towards centralization. Their ideal was 'assimilation'. Their colonial peoples would become French in culture and civilization, and send deputies to Paris to help govern the whole empire. 'Assimilation' seemed unattainable during the period of rapid expansion at the end of the nineteenth century and was accordingly modified, but it remained the ideal. The British preferred the policy of devolution. Different parts of the empire, especially the old colonies of settlement, were allowed varying degrees of autonomy. It was vaguely hoped that one day the whole empire might be coordinated in some form of federation. (Optimists, like Cecil Rhodes, even dreamt that the United States might be induced to rejoin such a federation.) In the newly acquired non-European territories, Britain experimented with various forms of 'indirect rule', which allowed the colonial peoples to govern themselves according to their customary laws and practices, with only a general oversight from British officials. The diversity of governmental practice adopted by the colonizing powers naturally influenced the form which decolonization was to take in different territories.

In one part of the British empire, India, there had always been a great deal of indirect rule, although it was not usually referred to by that title. Barely half of the Indian sub-continent was ever under direct British rule. The rest continued to be governed by the 'native princes', as they were collectively known, with British advisers. The American war of independence had convinced the British of the essentially transitory nature of empires. This was reinforced by their astonishment, as a small nation of northwestern Europe, at finding themselves the rulers of the Indian sub-continent. As late as 1838 Charles Trevelyan wrote: 'The existing connection between two such distant countries as England and India cannot, in the nature of things, be permanent: no effort of policy can prevent the natives from ultimately regaining their independence' (quoted in Stokes, 1959, p. 46). But he drew the same conclusion as Mountstuart Elphinstone, the Governor of Bombay, had drawn a decade earlier: 'It is for our interest to have an early separation from a civilized people, rather than a violent rupture with a barbarous nation, in which it is probable that all our settlers and even our commerce would perish, along with all the institutions we had introduced into the country' (Colebrooke, 1884, vol. 2, p. 72).

Such thinking lay behind the introduction of western education into India, which Mountstuart Elphinstone had admitted was Britain's 'high road back to Europe'. Trevelyan's brother-in-law, Thomas Babbington Macaulay, took up the same theme in his speech on the renewal of the East India Company's charter in 1833. In a famous peroration he told the Commons:

> It may be that the public mind of India may expand under our sys-
> tem till it has outgrown that system . . . that, having become in-
> structed in European knowledge, they may, in some future age,
> demand European institutions. . . . Whenever it comes, it will be
> the proudest day in English history. . . . The sceptre may pass away
> from us. . . . Victory may be inconstant to our arms. But there are
> triumphs which are followed by no reverse. There is an empire ex-
> empt from all natural causes of decay. Those triumphs are the pa-
> cific triumphs of reason over barbarism; that empire is the
> imperishable empire of our arts and our morals, our literature and
> our laws. (Quoted in Chamberlain, 1974, p. 71)

Even though during the imperialist period of the late nineteenth century the possibility of India becoming independent seemed indefinitely postponed, the same idea lay behind the slow introduction of some elements of representative government into India, beginning with the admission of a few nominated Indians to the Viceroy's Legislative Council under the Indian Council Act of 1861. Some further progress was made by the Government of India Act of 1909, usually known as the Morley–Minto reforms (after the Secretary of State for India, the veteran radical, John Morley, and the then Viceroy, Lord Minto), which provided for non-official (but not necessarily elected) majorities on the Legislative Councils of the Indian Provinces, although not yet on the Viceroy's own Legislative Council. Such advances seemed substantial at the time although they were modest enough even compared with the position already achieved by Britain's old colonies of settlement. Canada, Australia, South Africa and New Zealand had already obtained near autonomy in their domestic legislation and some, although still undefined, right to be consulted on foreign policy decisions which affected them. In other words, they had reached 'dominion status', which was defined for the first time in the 1907 Imperial Conference.

In 1914 the Dominions and India, as well as the British colonies, were automatically at war when Britain declared war on

Germany because, in international law, the British empire was still a single state. But the British government had already accepted in practice that the contribution to the war effort to be made by the Dominions and India would have to be determined in their respective capitals, rather than in London. The Dominions (South Africa less enthusiastically than the others) rallied to Britain's support. India too identified with the British cause and sent troops.

Britain, gratified by what seemed to be genuine loyalty on the Indian side, responded with the Montagu Declaration of 1917. Lord Montagu, the Secretary of State for India, announced on 20 August:

> The policy of His Majesty's Government . . . is that of the increasing association of Indians in every branch of the administration and the gradual development of self-governing institutions with a view to the progressive realization of responsible government in India as an integral part of the British empire.

It was a cautious statement with the emphasis on the word 'gradual', and this was further spelled out later in the text when Montagu emphasized that, since ultimate responsibility still lay with the British government, they must judge 'the time and measure of each advance' and this in turn would be determined by the degree of Indian 'co-operation'. But, hedged around though it was with provisos, the Montagu Declaration was still momentous. 'Self-governing institutions' and 'responsible government' were not vague phrases. In the development of relations between Britain and her colonies of settlement they had acquired precise legal meanings. What was being offered to India was 'dominion status', comparable to that already enjoyed by Canada, not immediately but in the foreseeable future. It was the first time that Britain had formally stated that this was the goal for any part of her 'non-white' empire. In the aftermath of the First World War it was, however, Germany, not Britain, which was the first European great power to be compelled to relinquish its pre-war empire. The American president, Woodrow Wilson, had hoped that at the end of the war there would be 'no annexations'. He did not wish to see any open wound left in Europe, such as that caused by the German annexation of Alsace-Lorraine after the Franco-Prussian war, but the Allies were equally determined not to return the German colonies, which had been captured in the course of the war. For the successor states of the Austro-Hungarian empire, which had collapsed at the end of the war, the Allies had committed themselves to the principle of 'self-determination'. The people themselves should choose to which state they would belong. New states, like Czechoslovakia and Yugoslavia, were created. Very tentatively, the Allies applied the same principle to the Ottoman (Turkish) empire which had also collapsed. During the war they had deliberately appealed for the support of the Arabs within the empire, many of whom were anxious to throw off Turkish rule. The Allies did not, however, yet judge these newly created Arab states to be capable of ruling themselves. It did not occur to any of the allied powers to apply the same principles of self-determination to Germany's, or their own, colonial empires. Colonial settlements were provided for in the fifth of President Wilson's famous Fourteen Points. The relevant clause demanded:

A free, open-minded and absolutely impartial adjustment of all colonial claims based upon a strict observance of the principle that in determining all such questions of sovereignty the interests of the populations concerned must have equal weight with the equitable claims of the government whose title is to be determined.

The Allies were somewhat embarrassed by the contrast between their proclaimed principles and the old-fashioned haggling over the fate of the former German colonies. The result was the establishment of the Mandate System, under the supervision of the new League of Nations organization. There were three classes of mandates. Class A mandates applied only to the successor states of the Ottoman empire. Syria and the Lebanon (until 1920 Lebanon was part of Syria) became French mandated territories. Iraq (Mesopotamia) and Palestine (which then included both the modern Israel and the modern Jordan) became British mandates. Class A mandates obligated the mandatory power not only to govern well, but to bring the mandated territory to full independence as soon as it reasonably could. Iraq became independent in 1932 but the others were still under the control of the mandatory powers when the Second World War broke out in 1939.

Class B and Class C mandates applied to the former German colonies in Africa and Asia. Class B mandates were granted to various European powers. Britain became responsible for Tanganyika (formerly German East Africa) and those parts of Togoland and the Cameroons that bordered her existing colonies of the Gold Coast and Nigeria. France took other parts of Togoland and the Cameroons which bordered her colonies of Dahomey and Gabon respectively. Class C mandates differed only slightly from Class B mandates but were granted to various African and Pacific powers. The Union of South Africa administered the former German South West (Namibia); Australia, part of New Guinea and various other Pacific islands; and New Zealand, Western Samoa. There was no formal obligation to advance these territories towards independence. The mandatory power was required only to provide good and humane government, to refrain from exploitation, and to suppress evils such as the remnants of the slave trade. The mandatory power was to send regular reports to the League of Nations Mandates Commission. The Commission took its work seriously. The mandatory powers were generally scrupulous in furnishing the reports and, so long as the League of Nations remained in existence, the Mandate System had at least the merit of setting standards, albeit paternalistic standards, by which the colonial powers might be expected to behave.

First Colonial Responses

Allied wartime propaganda, in particular the proclamation of the doctrine of self-determination, did not go unnoticed in the colonial world, particularly in those parts of it, such as British India, where there was already an educated and politically sophisticated class. The role of India is of peculiar importance in this story. There is now some debate among historians whether Africa should be regarded as simply following in the footsteps of Asia in her liberation struggles (Gifford and Louis, 1982, pp. vii–viii) . No doubt there is much in the African experience which is particular to Africa but the key role of the Indian nationalists can hardly be denied. Chief Awolowo of Nigeria wrote in 1945, 'India is the hero of the subject countries. Her struggles for self-government are keenly and sympathetically watched by colonial peoples'; although he was also aware of the terrible dangers of division between Hindu and Muslim, which could so easily be paralleled in Nigeria itself (Awolowo, 1947, pp. 25, 50–1). Many of the early nationalist movements in Africa deliberately adopted the name of Congress in imitation of the Indian National Congress. In 1912 in South Africa Pixley Seme, a young Zulu lawyer, who had been educated at Columbia and Oxford, called his new organization the South African Native National Congress. (It changed its name to the African National Congress, by which title it is known today, in 1925.) In 1918 a Gold Coast lawyer, J. E. Casely Hayford, founded the National Congress of British West Africa. Above all, India provided modern nationalist movements with a charismatic hero in Mahatma Gandhi, who seemed to combine an ability to use skilfully all the tactics of western politics with an authentic reaffirmation of non-European values. African leaders spoke of him with admiration (Nkrumah, 1957, pp. vii–viii). In 1969 Cyprus (independent since 1960) issued a stamp commemorating the centenary of his birth.

The first response of non-Europeans to the pressures of European conquest was naturally one of armed resistance. In the sixteenth century the Incas and the Aztec peoples of South and Central America had fought against the Spanish conquistadores. The Indians of North America went on fighting against the encroaching Europeans until the late nineteenth century. The battle of Wounded Knee between the Sioux Indians and the US cavalry was fought just before Christmas 1890 (Brown, 1972, p. 352).

In India the British and the French first gained political power as the auxiliaries of Indian rulers who were fighting over the inheritance of the crumbling Mogul empire but, as the British became contenders in their own right, they encountered fierce resistance from some indigenous claimants. Siraj-ud-daula, the nawab Bengal, failed to defeat the forces of the English East India Company at Plassey in 1757, but it was not until 1799 that Tipu Sultan, the ruler of Mysore in southern India, was defeated in the battle of Seringapatam by Arthur Wellesley, later Duke of Wellington and not until 1803 that Wellesley defeated the Maratha Confederation at the battle of Assaye. Some have contended that, but for the British intervention, the Marathas would have been the successors of the Moguls. The claim is not universally accepted (Spear, 1965, pp. 74–7, 116–17), but the Victorians did tend to date their own supremacy in India from the final defeat and dissolution of the Maratha Confederation in 1818.

Military resistance in India can be paralleled in Africa, particularly where the Europeans encountered a strong, and sometimes militaristic, state or empire. On the Gold Coast the British fought a series of wars in 1821–31, 1873–4, 1895–6 and 1900–1 against the powerful Ashanti Confederation. In South Africa they fought the Zulus in 1879, suffering at the outset the disastrous defeat of Isandhlwana. The Boer trekkers of course fought the Zulus over a much longer period of time. Zululand was incorporated into the British colony of Natal in 1897 but a major Zulu rebellion broke out in 1906. An offshoot of the Zulus, the Matabele (Ndebele), fought the British in 1893 to prevent them from establishing control of what was to become Southern Rhodesia (the modern Zimbabwe). More surprisingly, the Shona people, who had already been cowed by the Matabele and were expected to welcome the British as liberators, also rose against them in 1896. The British conquered Egypt in 1882 without much difficulty but were expelled from the Egyptian Sudan in 1885 by an Islamic fundamentalist, the Mahdi. They only regained control of the Egyptian Sudan as the result of a full-scale campaign under General Kitchener in 1896–8. The Italians failed to make good their bid for Abyssinia, suffering a humiliating defeat at the battle of Adowa in 1896. The French, expanding from their old colony of Senegal, fought their way through the Western Sudan, until they were finally checked by the British at Fashoda in 1898, against very fierce resistance from the well-organized Muslim emirates of the savannah belt. In the north it took the French nearly twenty years to subdue Algeria after their first landing there in 1830.

Nevertheless, all these attempts at military resistance ultimately failed. Even Abyssinia fell to the Italians in 1935. The simplest explanation for this, and one which obviously contains a great deal of truth, is the great disparity of power which by then existed between the Europeans and their opponents. By the late nineteenth century Europe had undergone an industrial revolution and the rest of the world had not. It was not only a question of military superiority, although Hilaire Belloc was right when he pointed out that the Europeans had the Maxim gun (a type of machine-gun) and their opponents did not. The Europeans also had far superior means of transport, including steamships, railways and, by the twentieth century, aircraft. They could overwhelm village output by factory production. They had all the efficient bureaucracy of the modern state at their command. The effects were psychological as well as material. Early African nationalists later wryly recalled their awe when they first encountered examples of European technology, such as a railway engine.

The peoples of India and China, with centuries of sophisticated civilization behind them, were less overwhelmed by the Europeans' self-proclaimed superiority. Tipu Sultan, for example, had a nice line in anti-British propaganda. Sometimes it would take a cruel turn as in his famous working model (now in the Victoria and Albert Museum) of a man-eating tiger devouring an English officer – the point being that the tiger was Tipu Sultan's personal emblem. When the British troops penetrated into his capital, Seringapatam, in 1799 they found caricatures on the walls, depicting red-faced Europeans sprawling drunkenly at or under tables, amid the dogs and the swine.

The Chinese, although defeated by the British in the so-called opium war of 1839–42 (in fact the war had as much to do with trade in general and with the British determination to make the Chinese conform to European norms of diplomacy as with opium), regarded their victorious enemies without awe. Commissioner Lin drafted a magisterial rebuke to the foreign invaders in 1839. He wrote:

> The Way of Heaven is fairness to all; it does not suffer us to harm others in order to benefit ourselves. . . . Your country lies twenty thousand leagues away; but for all that the Way of Heaven holds good for you as for us, and your instincts are not different from ours; for nowhere are there men so blind as not to distinguish between what brings life and what brings death, between what brings profit and what does harm. (Quoted in Waley, 1958, pp. 28–9)

For all that, the Chinese had to open the five 'treaty ports' to the invaders and, later in the century, grant an increasing number of concessions to various foreign powers. By about 1900 it seemed impossible that China would escape partition by Russia, Germany, Britain, France, Italy and the United States. It was not military power which saved her, although the Chinese did resist strenuously in 1839–42 and again in 1856–60. In 1900, avenging the attack on their embassies during the Boxer Rebellion, the armies of Britain, France, Germany, America and Japan reached and occupied the Chinese capital of Peking. China was saved partly by the watchful jealousy of the Great Powers, whose rivalry also kept the Ottoman empire intact until the First World War. But equally important was the surviving political unity of the country. China was not fragmented into many political units as was Africa. The dynasty was weak but not yet crumbling as was the Mogul empire when the British obtained control of India. The Chinese confidence in the virtues of their own civilization and their suspicion of, and contempt for, foreigners meant that there were very few 'collaborators' among the Chinese.

Collaborators were an essential element in the imposition of colonial rule. But, paradoxically, they also helped to generate those very forces which were ultimately to overthrow colonial governments.

This idea is interestingly worked out in Ronald Robinson's paper, 'Non-European foundations of European imperialism: sketch for a theory of collaboration' (Owen and Sutcliffe, 1972, pp. 117–40). The creation of a new 'westernized' class was particularly important in India and can he traced back before the 'Mutiny' of 1857.

1

The British Empire: Asia

India

The Indian Mutiny of 1857 belongs essentially to the first phase of colonial resistance. It was armed resistance, spearheaded by units of the Bengal army. The army had grievances of its own. Indian soldiers had willingly co-operated with the English East India Company in the squabbles over the spoils of the Mogul empire in the eighteenth century but, as the British grip on India tightened, they found that they were no longer allowed free rein to loot (the traditional way in which a soldier supplemented his pay) and that they were no longer promoted to the higher ranks. Elphinstone had prophesied as early as 1819, 'I think the seed of [our Indian empire's] ruin will be found in the native army – a delicate and dangerous machine which a little mismanagement may easily turn against us.' The supposed attack upon the soldiers' caste and religion, symbolized by the issue of the cartridges allegedly 'greased' with the fat of cows and pigs, was only the last straw. On the face of it, the 1857 rising should have succeeded. The British were numbered in thousands, the Indians in millions. Even the 'native' army outnumbered the British soldiers some five to one. The Mutiny failed, not only because it did not spread to the armies of Bombay and Madras but also because it failed to attract the support of many in Bengal. A hundred years later leading Indian historians came to regard it as a backward looking movement, trying to restore the old feudal India and so putting itself at odds with the forces of the future (Sen, 1957, p.

142). Westernized Indians held aloof from it and sometimes became its victims.

The British had fostered western-style education in India from the 1820s when, for example, the Elphinstone Institute, a great nursery for future nationalists, was founded in Bombay. A more definite decision in favour of western education was taken in 1835, supported by Macaulay's notorious 'education minute', deriding the traditional learning of India which, only a generation earlier, had been held in some respect in the West. Many Indians took enthusiastically to western education. When, in 1903, the then Viceroy, Lord Curzon, tried to check the proliferation of small colleges and to concentrate government subsidies on a few big institutions, like the University of Calcutta, it was regarded as a mortal insult by the Indian middle classes. There was, however, a marked difference in the 'take-up rate' of different communities. The Hindus were generally enthusiastic. The Muslims, who disliked seeing western secular education displace their own religious-based system, were not. As a result Muslims, who had been the governing class under the emperors, saw themselves pushed aside in favour of young Hindu clerks.

The British were quite aware that the Indians might apply to their own situation lessons learned from British history, which is not without its heroes in struggles against unlawful usurpation of authority. In fact the Indians noted not only the implications of the struggles between King and Parliament in seventeenth-century England but also those of the revolutions in Europe in 1848 and the intensification of Ireland's struggle against England. When the East India Company's charter came up for renewal in 1853 they, or at least a small number among them, were ready to organize themselves to lobby the British government. A remarkable meeting took place in Bombay in August 1852 which crossed all the usual religious boundaries, for it included Parsis, Muslims, Hindus and even Jews. They petitioned the British government for a number of studiously moderate reforms, including a larger share of administrative and judicial appointments for Indians. One of the leading spirits was Dadabhai Naoroji, a graduate of the Elphinstone Institute, who was later to sit in the British Parliament as MP for Finsbury. The Bombay Association, founded some five years before the Mutiny, was the voice of the new westernized India. These Indians were beginning to realize that using their conqueror's own political and philosophical weapons could be more effective than resorting to force of arms. The Bombay Association foreshadowed the Indian National Congress.

The Congress was established in 1885. The moving spirit was an Englishman, Alan Octavian Hume, the son of the British radical, Joseph Hume, and, at least at first, the Viceroy, Lord Dufferin, regarded it as an important means of ascertaining Indian opinion, and gave it his cautious encouragement. Some later Indian nationalists disliked the idea that what became the symbol and main instrument of Indian nationalism originated with an Englishman but in fact the Indian response was highly sophisticated. They saw it as a useful means of communicating their views to the British government through a body which, if not quite quasi-official, at least had official blessing and approval. For this reason they allowed it to supersede organizations like the Indian Association of Calcutta and the Indian National Conference, set up by Surendranath Banerjea a little earlier. Banerjea, at this time a lecturer at the University of Calcutta after a short and disastrous career in the Indian Civil Service, founded the Indian Association to be 'the centre of an All-India movement', based on 'the conception of a united India, derived from the inspiration of Mazzini'. He undertook a remarkable tour of Upper India, speaking at Agra, Delhi, Lahore, Alallabad, Benares and many other places in the Punjab and the United Provinces (as they were then called).

The significance of this was not lost on the more perceptive British officials (Majumdar, 1961, pp. 889–90). Something which could be called 'Indian nationalism' was emerging. This in itself was revolutionary. Whatever India was before the British period she was not a nation. Twice in her history, once under Asoka in the third century BC, and then under the Moguls, the greater part of the Indian sub-continent had been united under a single dynasty. But these always remained 'empires' rather than nation states. It is probably true to say that in the eighteenth century the sub-continent of India had less unity, ethnically, linguistically and culturally, than did the continent of Europe. Yet India (admittedly without Pakistan, which some Indians regarded as a border region, scarcely

Indian in character) emerged from the British period as a single nation and remains so more than a generation after independence.

Indian nationalism was forged during the British period. This was partly the result of material advances. The new railways, as well as the new postal system, made it possible for people in different parts of India to communicate with each other as never before. The possession of an official language, English, known to all the new educated men, was perhaps even more important. India has more than two hundred indigenous languages and English has become so vital as a lingua franca that even today it is one of the official languages of independent India. But, most crucial of all, the concept of nationalism was imported into India along with the rest of western learning. Nationalism, in the sense of a citizen owing a primary duty to a nation state, seems to be an entirely western concept. Loyalty to a group is, of course, a universal human characteristic but that can take many forms; loyalty to a family group or tribe, to a small political unit like a city, or to a very wide group like a religious faith. The primacy of loyalty to the state is a western concept and a fairly modern one at that. It can be found in medieval Europe, particularly in countries such as England, which achieved national unity early, but it did not evolve to its present form until the nineteenth century. But it was to prove easily the most successful ideological weapon that the colonized had against the colonizers.

From its beginning the Indian National Congress claimed to speak for the whole of India to the British authorities. Unfortunately, that claim was flawed. Congress was never an elected assembly or parliament, although it came to speak as if it was. It was more like a political party, which anyone could join on paying the membership fee. It was originally recruited by invitation from the graduates of the University of Calcutta. As a result it was at first drawn from a very narrow class of professional men. Those present at the early meetings of Congress were mostly lawyers and teachers, with a sprinkling of doctors and journalists. A more serious defect was that the Muslim community was grossly under-represented. There were only two Muslims present at the first session of Congress in 1885. The class bias to some extent righted itself as Congress became more broadly based after the First World War; but the religous bias was never really corrected and, in 1906, the Muslims set up their own organization, the Muslim League. Congress did not entirely satisfy even the Hindu community. The Untouchables complained that Congress only really represented the caste Hindus and paid scant attention to the Untouchables' grievances.

In its early days, until the First World War, Congress was in the main studiously moderate in its politics, calculating that the important thing was to retain the ear of the government. This was not, however, incompatible with some hard-hitting attacks on aspects of British policy. In particular, the British were blamed for aggravating the great problem of Indian poverty by 'draining' Indian money to London and by ruining Indian industries because of unrestrained competition from British factory production, especially in textiles. Congress asked for the further development of representative institutions in India but gave priority to the greater employment of Indians in the higher levels of the administration (Philips, 1962, pp. 151–6).

Indian nationalism in this period took two distinct forms, conveniently symbolized in two men, G. K. Gokhale and B. G. Tilak. Both as it happened were brahmins from the Bombay region but there the resemblance ended. Gokhale, sometimes called 'the Indian Gladstone', was very critical of British economic policy but he was prepared to work for liberal reforms gradually and through the official channels. He was respected by English politicians and particularly important for his influence on John Morley. Tilak saw his life's work as leading a great Hindu revival. He looked back to a rather mythical golden age, not only before the British raj but before the Muslim invasions. He rejected western education and western political concepts (although at times he used both). He saw the battle against poverty, which was important to the moderate party in Congress, as a distraction from the real task of purifying India and freeing her from the taint of foreign rule. Western politicians did not get on with Tilak, especially when he campaigned against the abolition of child marriages or vaccination against smallpox as attacks on Hindu tradition, and preached political assassination as a legitimate form of protest.

The First World War ended an epoch in Anglo-Indian relations. The British were gratified by Indian support. The Indians expected their reward. They were bitterly disappointed by the slowness of the British response. The Government of India Act of 1919 introduced the famous principle of 'dyarchy' by which some spheres, such as education and health, were 'transferred' to Indian control at the provincial level, while others such as public order were 'reserved' and remained under British control. The central government, removed in 1911 from Calcutta to New Delhi, remained firmly in British hands, even though the Legislative Assembly now had an elected majority. All this seemed quite inadequate to the Indians and they were further offended by the Rowlatt Acts, which retained some emergency wartime legislation, including the right in certain cases to detain individuals without trial.

In many parts of India protest campaigns began, including *hartals*, a kind of general strike. This unrest led to the Amritsar massacre of 13 April 1919. The Punjab had been a particular centre of disturbances and a number of Europeans had been attacked. The authorities were extremely nervous and full of memories of 1857. When General Dyer arrived at Amritsar on 11 April with a small force of troops, he immediately banned public meetings. Despite this a large crowd, including women and children, gathered on some waste ground known as the Jallianwala Bagh. Some undoubtedly assembled in deliberate defiance of the ban but many others had come in from the countryside for the annual horsefair, quite unaware of it. Dyer marched his troops of British and Indian soldiers to the Jallianwala Bagh and opened fire on the crowd without the usual warnings, deeming that his prohibition of meetings had been sufficient warning. Three hundred and seventy-nine people were killed and many more wounded. Dyer seems to have been unaware that the crowd could not disperse because his own troops were blocking the main exit. Amritsar sharply divided British and Indian opinion. An official inquiry under a Scottish judge, Lord Hunter, found against Dyer, but he received a great deal of support in the British press. Congress set up its own committee of inquiry which condemned Dyer much more sharply than Hunter had done, calling the deed 'a calculated piece of inhumanity'. Many young Indian nationalists, including Nehru, later said that it was Amritsar which finally turned them against the British. It may have done, but it was probably only the catalyst which finally crystallized their doubts.

A new generation of nationalist leaders was now emerging, Mohendas Karamchand Gandhi and Jawarharlal Nehru among them. Gandhi was undoubtedly the greatest of these new men in both Indian and international terms. He had been born in 1869 in the princely state of Porbandar in western India. His father and grandfather had both been prime ministers of that state. His family were devout Hindus, indeed his mother was a woman of exceptional piety. They may have been influenced by the Jain tradition which was strong in the neighbourhood and was notable for its strict pacifism. As a young man Gandhi came to London to study law at the Inner Temple. He left a touching account of his dilemmas at that time in his unfinished autobiography, *My Experiments with Truth*. On the one hand, like most educated young Indians, he very much wanted to identify with the British, even down to choosing the right tailor and taking dancing lessons; on the other, he wanted to keep his promises to his mother and remain faithful to his religion in matters such as not eating meat. Curiously, the latter promise led him to vegetarian restaurants and brought him into contact with the idealistic socialists of the day. In this period Gandhi was deeply impressed by some western writers such as Tolstoy, and by the ethical (although not the doctrinal) content of Christianity. He also discovered for the first time some of the great Sanskrit texts, reading them originally in English translations.

In 1893 Gandhi went to South Africa to practise as a lawyer, finding many of his clients among the sizeable Indian commumity. He came to hate the discrimination against Asians, as well as against the black Africans, which he found there. He established his first newspaper, *Indian Opinion*, in 1904 and began to work out his characteristic political doctrines, above all that of *satyagraha*. This, he admitted, would look to the outsider like mere civil disobedience or passive resistance; but he contended that such a view ignored the very positive spiritual content which he wished to see incorporated into it. Some laws were so unjust that to obey them was to become tainted with guilt yourself. The follower of *satyagraha* must normally be law-abiding but, on those rare occasions when his conscience compelled him to break the law, he must do so without violence. 'He then openly and civilly breaks them and quietly suffers the penalty for their breach.' The essence of the doctrine was that the suffering must be borne by the protesters, not inflicted upon others (Philips, 1962, pp. 215–16).

Angry though he was about the situation in South Africa, Gandhi was not at this time hostile to the British empire. Indeed he still identified with it and seems to have regarded South African practices as a perversion of the real spirit of the empire. During the Boer War of 1899–1901 and the Zulu rising of 1906 he formed an ambulance corps to help the British cause. He came to London during the First World War and tried to raise a similar corps from Indian students in London. He returned to India in 1915 with no particular intention of challenging the British. Only in February 1919 during the passage of the Rowlatt Acts did he launch a civil disobedience campaign. He called for a *hartal* throughout India on 6 April. In retrospect the British were inclined to hold him largely to blame for the events in the Punjab, including Amritsar.

The man who was to be Gandhi's lieutenant in India, Jawarharlal Nehru, was in many ways a contrast to his leader. A Kashmiri brahmin, Nehru was an aristocrat to his fingertips. His father, Motilal Nehru, was a wealthy and successful laywer and an Anglophile. The young Nehru was sent to Harrow and Cambridge where, unusually for a man of his background, he read science, although he too later turned to the law. Until he joined Gandhi in his political campaigns in the 1920s, he knew little first hand of Indian poverty. He had been influenced before the war by the Russo-Japanese conflict of 1904–5. Until then Nehru had accepted, as most westernized Indians did, that a period of tutelage from a European power was necessary before the backward countries of Asia would be ready to manage their own affairs and take their place in the modern world. But here was a different model. Japan alone among the powers of Asia seemed to have found an effective counter to western encroachment. She had kept the foreigners out, except as advisers. She had remodelled her whole political, economic and military systems along western lines and had humiliatingly defeated a great western power. It is not surprising that the young Nehru went out and bought all the books he could find on Japan. Twenty years later he became interested in another society which seemed to be pulling itself up by its own bootlaces, post-revolutionary Russia. He visited the Soviet Union for the first time in 1927. He was impressed by some of the things he saw but he also had many reservations. In working out his own ideas of state socialism later, he was prepared to borrow ideas from Russia as from elsewhere but he felt no commitment to the Soviet creed. Nevertheless, particularly in his economic policy, Nehru remained essentially a westerner. He was shocked by Indian poverty and wanted to cure it by economic development and progress, whichever model he chose to adopt.

Gandhi was a different and more complex man. There is truth in the claim that he managed to combine in his one person the appeal of both Tilak and Gokhale. He understood western politics well enough and could play the British at their own game, but he also wished to reassert distinctive Indian values. He was not prepared to accept the traditions of his own people uncritically. His most important break with tradition was in his attempt to secure a more tolerable life for the Untouchables. But in the eyes of the Indian peasants, he was a recognized type of Indian holy man. His renunciation of wealth and comfort, his simple dress and diet, his *ashram* at Ahmadabad, his daily toil at the spinning-wheel, commanded their respect. He was able to mobilize the Indian masses in his support in a way which would have been impossible for a more conventional politician like Nehru. Nehru did not always agree with his leader, but he never doubted that Gandhi was a greater man than he was, and seems to have been quite content to remain his lieutenant until Gandhi's death in 1948.

The British had little idea how to deal with Gandhi. His first civil disobedience campaign broke down in violence and in 1922 Gandhi himself was arrested and sentenced to six years in gaol. His judge, Mr Justice Broomfield, made a remarkable statement to the prisoner in the dock, acknowledging that he was unlike any man he had ever tried before or was ever likely to try again, and that in the eyes of his own people he was not only a patriot but a saint. The judge dropped a broad hint to the authorities that Gandhi should be released as soon as the troubles died down (Philips, 1962, pp. 222–4). In fact Gandhi was released in 1924. In 1930 he led another great campaign of civil disobedience against the government salt monopoly, leading a march from his *ashram* to the sea at Dandi two hundred miles away, to pick up sea salt illegally from the shore.

Meanwhile the British were slowly plodding on with their plans to introduce representative and responsible government to India by instalments. The Simon Commission, a British parliamentary commission under the eminent lawyer, Sir John Simon, sat from 1927 to 1930. The fact that no Indian sat on it caused an outcry in India and was regarded as slightly absurd even in Britain, although technically it was a parliamentary body on which only members could sit. In an attempt to remedy this the British government invited representatives of various interests in India to meet representatives of the British Parliament in London at the so-called Round Table Conference, which met in three sessions in 1930, 1931 and 1932. Unfortunately, for a variety of reasons, many of the leading Indian figures were absent from the first and third sessions. The second was more generally representative but it only served to highlight the deep fissures which were now apparent in Indian society. Gandhi, as the representative of Congress, claimed to speak for the whole of India. His claim was sharply denied by M. A. Jinnah for the Muslim League and by Dr Ambedkar for the Untouchables.

One of the MPs on the Simon Commission was Clement Attlee, later to be prime minister of Britain's first majority Labour government in 1945–51. Attlee was deeply interested in Indian problems, and the Labour movement in general was a good deal more sympathetic to Indian aspirations than were the Conservatives. Keir Hardie had visited India in 1907 and been appalled at the poverty of the Indian peasants. Ramsay Macdonald, who was prime minister in the minority Labour governments of 1924 and 1929 (and the man who called the Round Table Conference), had visited India in 1909 and subsequently written a book, *The Awakening of India*, which anticipated some of the reforms offered to the Indians in the Government of India Act of 1935.

The Act of 1935 looked to a federal solution of India's difficulties, bringing in the princely states as well as the provinces of British India. There was to be some measure of responsible government at the centre, although foreign affairs and defence were still not transferred to Indian control. (Responsible government here meant that individual ministers would be answerable to the Legislative Assembly.) The eleven provinces were to have autonomous governments with ministries wholly responsible to elected legislatures, although the provincial governors still had considerable emergency powers. The Act was anathema to the more extreme Conservatives like Winston Churchill and Lord Salisbury, who fought it every step of the way. Indeed their opposition may well have delayed the passage of the measure from 1933 to 1935. This was to prove of crucial importance because it had been provided that the clauses relating to the central government should not become operative until at least 50 per cent of the rulers of the princely states had adhered. They had not done so by 1939 and so, as far as her central government was concerned, India entered the Second World War under the now totally obsolete constitution of 1919.

The 1935 Act had been brought into operation in the provinces and elections held in 1937. Congress had a spectacular success in the elections, winning six of the eleven provinces outright and emerging as the largest party in two more. It had originally intended to fight the elections only to prove its strength and then to decline to take office but the chance of real power, to put into operation some of the reforms it had so long been advocating, persuaded it to form ministries in the seven provinces where it had majorities. The Muslim League was chastened by its comparative lack of success – it had achieved respectable results only in Bengal, the Punjab and Sind – and made overtures to Congress. Congress, however, flushed with victory was in no mood to compromise. In October 1937 Jinnah abandoned any hope of co-operating with Congress. For the first time the creation of a separate Muslim state – first suggested in 1933 but not then taken very seriously – became a real political possibility.

The Indian response to the outbreak of the Second World War in 1939 was very different from that of 1914. Indians resented the fact that the British government had declared war on their behalf, although in strict international law that was unavoidable. Far from rallying to the British side Congress saw, as the Irish had so long done, Britain's difficulties as its opportunity. The Congress ministries in the provinces resigned and on 10 October the All-India Congress Committee resolved that 'India must be declared an independent nation' and demanded that India's future constitution must be determined by an Indian constituent assembly. The British could only reply that all major constitutional changes must wait until after the war. In 1940 France fell and Britain awaited probable invasion. By a supreme irony Winston Churchill, the Indian nationalists' old enemy, became British Prime Minister, while their former champion, Clement Attlee, became the Deputy Prime Minister.

But essentially the British and Indian attitudes remained unchanged throughout the war. The British insisted that nothing could be decided until the war was over; the Indians demanded immediate independence. The British negotiating position became weaker with the entry of Japan into the war in December 1941. Within months the Japanese had overrun Malaya and Burma. On 15 February 1942 the great naval base of Singapore surrendered and thousands of British troops were made captive, in some ways the most shattering British defeat of the war. The way to India seemed wide open. In these inauspicious circumstances Sir Stafford Cripps, an austere man of the left, was despatched to India in March 1942. It was hoped that he could win Gandhi's confidence but he had little new to offer – some extra Indian participation in government immediately, major changes at the end of the war. In the British view these changes contained all that the Indians could reasonably ask – a constituent assembly with the British pledged in advance to accept its conclusions even if they included secession from the Commonwealth. But they felt compelled to insist that there must be certain guarantees for racial and religious minorities and, in particular, that each province should be free to join the Indian union or not as it wished. Negotiations went on for seventeen days but in the end they broke down. The communal problem was still the great stumbling block. Congress feared that the Muslims might carry the Punjab, or even Bengal, out of the Indian state, even though both provinces had large Hindu minorities. For the rest of the war, the British continued to offer the Cripps proposals, Congress to reject them.

Gandhi was not sure that it was worth negotiating with the British any longer. He said that he was not interested in a 'post-dated cheque on a failing bank'. On 8 August 1942 the All-India Congress Committee passed the famous 'Quit India' resolution which, although promising an alliance to continue the war against the Japanese, demanded an immediate end to British rule and threatened that, if this demand was rejected, there would be `a mass struggle'. The British were not impressed. On 9 August the most prominent Congress leaders were arrested. There were sporadic disturbances and acts of sabotage, but the promised mass struggle did not materialize.

The Indians were in fact divided in their feelings about the war, now that it was on their doorstep. Some Indians, it is true, joined the Japanese 'Indian National Army' and prepared to march with the Japanese to 'liberate' India, but the Indian leaders were on the whole more cautious. They had no interest in merely exchanging masters and seeing the Japanese in the place of the British.

The war in Europe came to an end in May 1945, that in Asia three months later with the dropping of the atomic bombs on Hiroshima and Nagasaki. A general election in Britain gave a landslide victory to the Labour party led by Clement Attlee. On the face of it the British negotiating position was stronger than it had been in 1940–2, when they had their backs to the wall in Europe. In fact, appearances were deceptive. The British economy was nearly ruined by the war. Britain was now heavily dependent on American aid, and the United States was not in the least sympathetic to the continuation of the British empire in India.

Ideologically, the new government was committed to speedy independence for India but the practical obstacles were still formidable. In the spring of 1946 the Cabinet Mission of Lord Pethick Lawrence, Sir Stafford Cripps and A. V. Alexander went out to seek a basis for a settlement with the Indian leaders and to convince them that, since the British really were going to withdraw, they must reach agreement among themselves. They came near to success with a proposal for a federal form of government; but first Congress, then Jinnah, rejected it.

Jinnah decided that the Muslim League must show its strength and declared 16 August 1946 'Direct Action Day'. He subsequently claimed that he had expected only demonstrations, but the line between demonstrations and violence is often a thin one; and on 16 August something like four thousand people died, mainly in

Calcutta. The Viceroy, Lord Wavell, told Attlee that Britain must either resign herself to staying in India for at least another ten years and commit the resources to do so, or fix a date for withdrawal and stick to it, even if this meant handing over power to the only viable authorities, the provincial governments. Attlee rejected this as a counsel of despair and quite impracticable. He recalled Wavell and replaced him by Lord Mountbatten, who enjoyed all the prestige of the successful commander-in-chief of the last stages of the war in South-East Asia. But, at the end of the day, Mountbatten could only agree with Wavell's stark alternatives. The first was deemed impossible. There remained only the alternative of setting a date. On 20 February 1947 Attlee announced that, come what might, the British would leave India in June 1948.

A speedy withdrawal meant that partition had to be accepted. It could not be a satisfactory solution. The Muslim population was concentrated in the north-west and the north-east but Muslim communities were scattered all over India, making up between a fifth and a quarter of the whole population. In most cases the boundaries of existing provinces could be used for the new national boundaries of India and Pakistan, but Bengal and the Punjab had to be partitioned between them. The irrigation system of the Punjab had to be severed to the detriment of both parts. East Bengal became East Pakistan. It was separated by over a thousand miles from the larger West Pakistan. It was essentially an agricultural hinterland, producing cotton, tea and jute, and, cut off from its processing plants and export ports, now in West Bengal, it was scarcely viable.

In June Mountbatten announced on behalf of the British government that independence would in fact be brought forward from June 1948 to August 1947. The formal transfer of power took place on 14 August 1947. Many details had still not been worked out. It is possible that the British government thought that they could safely be left because the two new states would in practice be compelled to act as a quasi-federation along the lines of the Mission's proposals. If that was so, the British gravely miscalculated. Any hope of co-operation between India and Pakistan perished in the communal violence of the autumn of 1947. Although most of it was confined to the two partitioned states of Bengal and the Punjab, it there reached appalling proportions. Perhaps half a million died. About five million Muslims fled to Pakistan and about the same number of Hindus to India. More than twelve million were made homeless. Gandhi himself went to the Punjab in a desperate attempt to quell the violence, only to be assassinated himself in January 1948 by a Hindu fanatic.

Britain granting independence to India was the first major example of a country which had not been militarily defeated relinquishing an important overseas possession after the Second World War. On the face of it, it was a disaster, ending in partition and bloodshed. But this is not the whole story. It is true that Pakistan, like many other ex-colonies, has found it difficult to sustain a democratic form of government. It first came under military rule in 1958 and again, after a brief return to elected government, in 1977. Martial law lasted until 1985 and there was further military intervention in government in 1993. Separatist and bitter religious conflicts remain. East Pakistan seceded from West Pakistan and assumed the name Bangladesh in 1971.

India, on the other hand, proved to have much more stability than was apparent in 1947. More than a generation later it remains a democracy, the largest in the world. For forty years the Congress Party, which grew out of the Indian National Congress, dominated Indian politics but when it was defeated in an election in 1977, it left office and did not return until it won the election of 1980. Its power weakened in the 1990s. The election of February 1998 was inconclusive and allowed the formation of a coalition government, in which the strongest part was the BJP, a Hindu traditionalist party, feared by Muslims, Christians and other minority groups for its programme of departing from the strictly neutral secular state established in 1947.

Independent India's first prime minister, Nehru, emerged as a major world statesman. There were those who alleged that he did not practise the high-minded doctrines that he preached. In 1947 the princely states had been left to decide whether they would join India or Pakistan; but Hyderabad, which had a Muslim ruler but a Hindu majority, was incorporated into India virtually by force in 1949. Nehru was extremely reluctant to see Kashmir (where the reverse was true, a Hindu ruler and a Muslim majority) join Pakistan, and India and Pakistan fought three wars about its fate. An interim partition was accepted by both sides in the Simla Agreement of 1972 but was rejected by Kashmiri separatists, who have since waged an increasingly violent war against the Indian authorities. In 1961 the Portuguese enclave of Goa on the west coast of India was forcibly taken over. Nevertheless, Nehru developed a distinctive foreign policy of non-alignment during the Cold War and so gave a lead to the growing number of Asian and African countries which did not want to be drawn into the power struggles of East and West.

The connection between Britain and India was a long one, much longer than that between Britain and most of her colonies. India was also by far the most important of Britain's overseas possessions. Once it had gone, the *raison d'etre* for retaining an empire at all seemed much weaker. The most immediate impact of Britain's relinquishment of her Indian empire was naturally felt in the rest of Asia.

Ceylon, Burma and Malaya

Ceylon (Sri Lanka) has always been seen as a pendant to the Indian empire. The British had acquired it from the Dutch as a result of the Napoleonic wars. As in India the British had to face the problem of dealing with a majority and a minority community, the Sinhalese and the Tamils. On the whole they were rather proud of their record in Ceylon. It was a smaller, more manageable problem than in India, and was economically prosperous with its exports of tea and rubber. Unlike India, which was always a special case and was dealt with by first the Board of Control and later the India Office, not the Colonial Office, Ceylon was a conventional Crown Colony, ruled by a governor, assisted by an executive and a legislative council. Since 1923 Ceylon had enjoyed an unusually wide franchise and an elected majority in the Legislative Council. It became independent so smoothly on 4 February 1948, that the event received little international attention. But ethnic tensions increased in the 1980s, culminating in the guerrilla and terrorist activities of the Tamil Tigers.

Burma, even more than Ceylon, had in British eyes never been more than an outlying province of the Indian empire, conquered in three wars in 1824–6, 1852–3 and 1885–6. The Burmese had not accepted British rule willingly. Guerrilla warfare, dismissed by the British as dacoity, or brigandage, continued for many years. No doubt this helps to explain why some Burmese were willing to co-operate with the Japanese when they overran the country early in 1942. The Japanese set up a nominally independent state in Burma under a Burmese lawyer, Aung San. Aung San, however, saw himself as a national leader, not a mere quisling, and in 1944 he changed sides and offered his co-operation to the British. The Fourteenth Army painfully recovered Burma from the Japanese in 1944–5, but the British government had no real interest in restoring colonial rule. General elections after the war gave Aung Sun an overwhelming mandate for independence. Aung Sun himself was assassinated, with many of his ministerial colleagues, in July 1947 by political opponents; but he was succeeded by his former Foreign Secretary, Thakin Nu, and Burma became independent on 4 January 1948. Unlike India, Pakistan and Ceylon, Burma did not choose to remain within the British Commonwealth of Nations after independence. It has been under military rule since 1962. In 1989 it changed its name to Myanmar on the grounds that 'Burma' referred only to part of the country (although the name Burma is still often used, much as the Netherlands is often incorrectly referred to as Holland).

Malaya meant more to the British than did Burma. They had acquired it gradually. In 1819 Sir Stamford Raffles had obtained the island of Singapore from the Sultan of Johore. It had developed into a great entrepôt port and the most important British naval base in Asia. Singapore, the island of Penang and the mainland territory of Malacca came to form the Straits Settlements, originally under the control of the East India Company but transferred to the Colonial Office in 1867. The rest of the Malayan Peninsula consisted of princely states. None was formally a British colony. The Federated Malay States – Perak, Selangor, Negri Sembilan and Pahang – gradually fell under British control and administration between 1874 and 1896. The other five states, Kedah, Kelantan, Trengganu, Johore and Perlis, were under the suzerainty of Thailand until 1909 when they too passed under a British protectorate.

Malaya was a very important supplier of both rubber and tin. In the difficult days after the Second World War, Malaya's exports were vitally important in keeping the Sterling Area solvent. (The Sterling Area was formed in 1939 to maintain the pound sterling as an international currency. It included the whole of the British empire and Commonwealth – except Canada – and a few other countries.)

The Malayans, anxious to resume their independence, had first to face an unexpected challenge from communist guerrillas, mainly Chinese, who were anxious to acquire control of such essential raw materials. The Chinese were a minority community in Malaya and not popular. The Malayans had no desire to fall under the control of their great near neighbour, communist China. They were quite willing to accept the assistance of British forces under Field Marshal Templer. Templer fought a text-book campaign and expelled the guerrillas. In some ways Templer's success misled the British, and later the Americans. They came to believe that guerrillas could be defeated fairly easily by well-planned military action. Malaya, however, was unlike Cyprus or Vietnam. In Malaya the guerrillas were the enemies, not the allies, of the people.

After the defeat of the communists, Malaya proceeded quietly to independence. The Malayans united behind the Tunku, Abdul Rahman. Abdul Rahman was the kind of courteous conservative with whom the British had always felt able to do business. The Federation of Malaya became an independent state within the Commonwealth on 31 August 1957. On 16 September 1963 it was enlarged by the addition of Singapore (which had remained separate in 1959), Sabah (the former British North Borneo) and Sarawak, and adopted the name of Malaysia. Singapore, however, opted to resume its independence from the Federation on 9 August 1965. Brunei, the last British possession in the area, became independent in February 1984.

2

The British Empire: Africa

The African nationalists may have looked to the Asian precedents but the British government originally envisaged a very different time-scale for their African possessions. Discounting the Union (from 1961 the Republic) of South Africa, there were two main types of British colony in Africa. First, there were those with no appreciable white settler element. These included all Britain's West African colonies – the Gambia, Sierra Leone, the Gold Coast and Nigeria – and most of those in the eastern half of the continent – Uganda, Tanganyika, Zanzibar and Nyasaland. Northern Rhodesia was usually regarded as falling in the same class, although there was a larger European population there (73,000 in 1959). The two where the settler population was too important to be ignored were Kenya and Southern Rhodesia. Apart from these colonies, properly so-called, Britain controlled Egypt and the Egyptian Sudan.

African culture and civilization tended to be denigrated by Europeans until very recently. As late as 1963 the distinguished historian Hugh Trevor Roper (later Lord Dacre) could say in a television broadcast, 'Perhaps in the future there will be some African history to teach. But at present there is none: there is only the history of Europeans in Africa' (*Listener*, 1963, p. 871). He did at least concede that the ignorance might be on the European side and that African history might be 'discovered'. Many of his predecessors would simply have assumed, as did Sir Alan Burns, a notable and in many ways enlightened colonial administrator, that Africa had no history as Europe understood the term; he wrote, 'For countless centuries, while all the pageant of history swept by,

Africa remained unmoved in primitive savagery.' In fact, since the Second World War, a very different picture has emerged of African history and its place in the world; but this came too late to have much influence on those who had to take the vital decisions about decolonization. They almost universally saw Africa as 'backward' and African nationalism as in its infancy compared to the mature and clamant nationalism of Asia.

Most of Africa had been partitioned between the European powers in the seven or so years between the Berlin West Africa Conference of 1884–5 and the long series of treaties between European powers tidying up colonial boundaries in 1890–1. Most of British Africa was decolonized in an equally short space of time between the independence of the Gold Coast (Ghana) in 1957 and the independence of Nyasaland (Malawi) and Northern Rhodesia (Zambia) in 1964. When so much territory was acquired so quickly during the Scramble for Africa in the 1880s the British government had neither wished, nor been able, to provide effective administration for all of it – although the terms of the Berlin Act at the end of the conference required some show of European presence in order to establish a valid claim to a region. The British at first governed many of these territories as protectorates under the Foreign Office, not colonies under the Colonial Office; and left some of them – Nigeria, East Africa (Kenya and Uganda) and the Rhodesias – to the control of chartered companies. All except Southern Rhodesia, however, eventually became normal colonies under the jurisdiction of the Colonial Office.

The last thing the British Treasury, or the British taxpayer, wished to do was to commit large sums of money to the development of these colonies. Ironically for those who have contended that 'surplus capital' seeking a home abroad drew Britain into her late-nineteenth-century expansion of empire, capitalists were generally reluctant to invest in the African colonies. When Joseph Chamberlain was at the Colonial Office he secured the passage of the Colonial Loans Act in 1899, to make it easier for colonial governments to borrow money for necessary developments; but not until 1929 was an Act passed, the Colonial Development Act, which actually committed government money for works in the colonies. This was overtaken by the Slump and, by 1938, only four million pounds had been allocated to the British colonies in Africa. The Second World War saw two new Acts, the Colonial Development and Welfare Acts of 1940 and 1945. It is not entirely correct to see these as the direct result of the war, since they had been under discussion before and were part of the general new thinking about the management of the economy provoked by the economic disasters of the 1930s – new thinking which was sometimes interrupted, sometimes accelerated by the war. But, by 1945, the British government had recognized an obligation to finance the development of social services such as health and education in the British colonies, as well as trying to lay economic foundations. Before the war education in the British colonies had been largely in the hands of private enterprise, which for the most part meant the missionaries. They had to face much the same problems as the government had had to face in India. Should they provide English or vernacular education? Should they concentrate on primary education for as many people as possible or aim rather to educate an elite, who might then be expected to act as the educators of the rest of their people, the 'leaven in the lump' theory? They did not give consistent answers to these questions but on the whole they favoured western-style education, partly because of their belief in the poverty of African civilization as an alternative. In Nigeria this led them into the same difficulties as they had encountered in India. The Islamic emirates of Northern Nigeria had no wish to substitute western education for their own system. The Ibos of southern Nigeria on the other hand being politically fragmented and not attached to one of the world's great religious systems, took readily to western education and so came to provide the clerks and civil servants for the administration – and were soon to be bitterly resented in the North.

This was one example of the unintentional revolution which colonial intervention could cause in traditional societies. All British colonies saw the rise of a new western educated middle class, which might well find itself at odds with traditional authorities. The situation was further complicated when the British were also relying, as they were in Nigeria, on a system of 'Indirect Rule', which involved close co-operation with the old authorities. Thomas Hodgkin described the inherent contradictions in British policy between:

the conception of 'Indirect Rule', i.e. of local government as resting in the hands of the traditional rulers – Native Authorities – operating within the framework of a British controlled administration: the system depending for its success upon relations of sympathy and mutual respect between British administrator and African chief [and] the progressive weakening of the influence of the traditional rulers, with the rise of an African middle class, whose status depends on wealth and education, not on lineage: who tend to reject traditional authority as unenlightened, incompetent and British-inspired; and who, as a politically conscious, pushing bourgeoisie, tend to be regarded with less sympathy and respect by the administrator than the 'non-political' gentlemanly chief. (Hodgkin, 1956, p. 46)

The British did not concentrate on practical and vocational education to the same extent as the Belgians in the Congo; even so, with only three exceptions (Fourah Bay Teachers' Training College in Sierra Leone, Achimota in the Gold Coast and Makerere in Uganda), the education available in the British colonies did not go beyond the secondary level until after the Second World War. Only when independence began to seem fairly imminent were university colleges established in the Gold Coast, Nigeria, Uganda and the Sudan. Between the wars young Africans who wished to proceed to higher education had to go to Europe or America. Nmandi Azikiwe of Nigeria got to the United States in 1925 by the simple expedient of stowing away on a ship, and studied at various American universities, including the University of Pennsylvania and Lincoln University, a famous centre of Black studies. Kwame Nkrumah of Ghana also studied at Lincoln and Pennsylvania between 1935 and 1945. He returned home by way of London and spent some time at the London School of Economics, where he met the veteran British socialist, Professor Laski. Jomo Kenyatta of Kenya also studied at the LSE in the 1930s under the anthropologist, Professor Malinowski. In 1930 Kenyatta himself published a book, *Facing Mount Kenya*, which was hailed as important as the first major anthropological study by an African, writing of a society he knew from the inside.

Receipt of higher education abroad, although it was forced upon them, brought benefits to the first generation of African nationalists. They came into contact with eminent Europeans who were sympathetic to their cause. Men from different British colonies in both West and East Africa met one another in London or America. The artificial boundaries of the colonial period seemed absurd to them and the idea of pan-Africanism was born. They also met black Americans.

This last point was to be crucial. Black Americans were beginning to take an interest in their own past and so in Africa. The movement began in the middle of the nineteenth century when Edward Blyden, a West Indian who moved to Liberia in 1850, started to write with pride of the African race and tried to persuade others to develop a similar consciousness (July, 1968, pp. 208–33). Another influential West Indian was Marcus Garvey, who preached a doctrine of 'Africa for the Africans' and advised black Americans to return to their motherland – thus ironically winning the support of some white racialists. Some looked askance at Garvey's willingness to advocate the use of force, but he influenced the thinking of Kwame Nkrumah.

From an organizational point of view, the key name was that of an American, W. E. B. Du Bois, who had written, among other things, an important history of the slave trade. His great dream was a pan-African movement which would embrace both American and African Negroes. In 1919 he organized, with the help of the Sengalese, Blaise Diagne, a Pan-African Conference which met in Paris in the hope of influencing the deliberations of the Peace Conference then meeting there. It in fact had little impact on the decisions of the assembled statesmen, but a 'Pan-African Conference' continued to meet at irregular intervals between the wars. Until the Second World War they were dominated by the Americans.

The fifth/sixth Pan-African Conference which met in Manchester in 1945 was different. It was a large gathering of over two hundred delegates. A number of leading African nationalists, including Nkrumah and Kenyatta, were present. It was also much more radical in temper. The delegates unanimously endorsed 'the doctrine of African socialism based upon the tactics of positive action without violence'. In short, it had undergone something of the same transformation which had taken place in the Indian National Congress after the First World War. It now saw itself as a fighting body, ready to confront the colonial powers.

The British government was no longer disposed to dispute the principle of the transfer of power to African states. The controversy centred entirely on how quickly and by what stages the transfer was to be made. On political, as on economic, questions British thinking had already begun to alter before the war. The two matters were in fact connected. A more active development programme was likely to imply the need both for more efficient government and for the more active consent of the governed. 'Native Authorities' might not be adequate for this. In Professor Hargreaves's memorable phrase they were like 'vintage cars, elaborate and dignified structures with little capacity for acceleration, and strong tendencies to steer to the right' (Hargreaves, 1979, p. 25). The association of middle-class Africans, the 'new men', with government had its risks from the British point of view but it had to be faced. In 1938 Lord Hailey, a former member of the Indian Civil Service, published his magisterial *African Survey*, commissioned by the Royal Institute of International Affairs, in which he discussed, among other things, the relationship between indirect rule and representative government.

At the end of 1939 Hailey was sent out by the Colonial Office to look further into this. The Colonial Office explained this to the governors of the British West African colonies: 'It may be that one of the results of the war will be to stimulate the political consciousness of Africans and to give emphasis to the demand for a quickened pace of development towards more representative and liberal institutions of government' (Hargreaves, 1979, p. 27). Hailey presented his conclusions in a report, *Native Administration and Political Development in British Tropical Africa*, which was widely circulated in the Colonial Office, although it was not published until 1953. Hailey did not doubt that the colonies were entering a phase of 'rapid change'. His advice was detailed and subtle. He had little faith in 'constitution-mongering' but preferred to try to identify potential political and administrative elites who could be trained to assume the responsibilities of government. Some hint of the new British thinking was conveyed to the Americans in the series of lectures which Hailey gave at Princeton in 1943.

It was, by then, necessary to try to win American sympathy. The climate of world opinion on the morality of colonialism changed much more sharply during the Second World War than during the First. The European colonial powers could assume that nothing in President Wilson's Fourteen Points was directed at them. But there were many who thought that the Atlantic Charter, agreed between Britain and America in August 1941 on common objectives, was essentially incompatible with colonialism. The United Nations Charter was certainly difficult to reconcile with it; significantly the Pan-African Conference at Manchester in 1946 specifically endorsed the United Nations Declaration of Human Rights.

Ghana

The Gold Coast was the first British colony in Black Africa chosen for independence – and there was an element of conscious experiment.

The Gold Coast had a longer tradition than most colonies of African participation in the colonial government, and also of African protest movements. As early as 1888 two Africans were nominated to the Legislative Council which assisted the British Governor at Cape Coast Castle, a modest enough beginning. But, in fact, Africans held more administrative posts in Britain's West African colonies in the nineteenth century than they did in the early twentieth. (A striking example from Church, not State, is that the first Anglican bishop of the Niger, Samuel Crowther, was a Yoruba ex-slave.) In the nineteenth century West Africa was still regarded as the 'white man's grave' and few Europeans wished to undertake duties there. As medical science improved the Europeans became less reluctant and tended to displace Africans in the administration. In 1897 a number of Gold Coast chiefs formed the Aborigines' Rights Protection Society to safeguard their position, but the first recognizably modern political association was Casely Hayford's National Congress of British West Africa at the end of the First World War.

Between the wars the Gold Coast became quietly prosperous. Its agriculture, organized on a peasant proprietor system, quite unlike the plantation farming which was emerging in East Africa, found an excellent cash crop in cocoa. After the Second World

War it was the world's most important producer and, together with Malaya, kept the Sterling Area solvent. The Gold Coast had a larger middle class than most African states and was able to spend more on education and health than its neighbours. It was extraordinarily bad luck that on the very eve of independence, the cocoa crop was infected with a fungus disease and the economy badly disrupted.

The Second World War saw a certain amount of what Lord Hailey had contemptuously dismissed as 'constitution-mongering'. Immediately after the war in 1946 a new constitution, the Burns constitution (Sir Alan Burns was then Governor), was introduced. It gave an elected African majority on the Governor's Council, a concession which was looked upon as very advanced. At that time the only other British colonies with non-European majorities (discounting India) were Ceylon and Jamaica. The Executive Council had remained an entirely official body, although since 1942 it had included nominated Africans. The new constitution was expected to usher in a period of consolidation.

Even when J. B. Danquah formed his United Gold Coast Convention in 1947 to work for changes in the constitution, the government was not very worried. Danquah's party was a moderate group of professional and business men, who wanted a smooth transition of political power to African hands, including those of the traditional authorities, without altering the structure of society. The situation changed when Kwame Nkrumah was invited to come from London to become the secretary of the new party. Nkrumah himself hesitated, realizing that his own views were very different from those of Danquah. His thinking was now very radical. While in London he had met a number of leading British communists, including Harry Politt, Palme Dutt and Emil Burns. He helped to set up the 'West African National Secretariat', with an office in the Gray's Inn Road as a meeting place for African and West Indian students, which for a short time published a newspaper, the *New African*; but he was also a member of an inner group called 'The Circle', which aimed to start revolutionary activities anywhere in Africa (Nkrumah, 1957, pp. 55, 60)

On his return to the Gold Coast Nkrumah began to tour the country organizing the party. When serious rioting broke out in Accra in February 1948 and spread to Kumasi and other towns, suspicion immediately fell on Nkrumah. Casualties were officially estimated at 29 dead and 237 injured. When the authorities found a Communist Party card and a document outlining the aims of 'the Circle' in Nkrumah's possession they felt that their suspicions were amply justified. Colin Cross compares the Accra riots to the fall of the Bastille (Cross, 1968, p. 270). The comparison may not be exact, but the riots did shake the British government out of any complacent supposition that a small instalment of constitutional reform would satisfy the Africans for the foreseeable future. A committee of enquiry under a KC, Mr Aiken Watson, reported in June 1948 that the Burns constitution must already be regarded as obsolete. A new committee with an all-African membership under an African judge, Mr Justice Coussey, worked out a new constitution.

In the summer of 1949 Nkrumah broke with the UGCC and founded his own Convention People's Party. He had already gained the support of the so-called 'Youth Section' of the UGCC. (Youth is a word which must be treated with caution in an African context at this time. It tended to mean the new men with western skills, rather than teenagers.) He now went all out for mass support, especially from the trade unions. The youth sections (sometimes also rather loosely referred to as 'students') and the trade unions were the key to many African nationalist movements. Nkrumah began to organize a campaign of what he called 'Positive Action', by which he meant agitation, strikes, boycotts and general non-cooperation on a Gandhian model.

In January 1950 he was arrested and subsequently sentenced to three years' imprisonment on various charges of sedition. He thus joined the ranks of the 'prison graduates', who so often came straight into power on independence. No one seems to have tried seriously to stop Nkrumah from organizing his party from within prison. When elections were held under the Coussey constitution in February 1951, the CPP emerged as the strongest single party.

The new Governor, Sir Charles Arden-Clarke, was genuinely committed to swift progress towards self-government. He ordered Nkrumah's immediate release from prison and invited him to take the post of 'Leader of Government Business' – the name was not changed to prime minister until March 1952.

Nkrumah, according to his autobiography, was well aware of

the practical difficulties before him. The Gold Coast lacked enough trained Africans to take over immediately from the colonial authorities. The economic difficulties resulting from the disease of the cocoa crop were serious. The country had a desperate need of foreign investment for vital schemes such as the Volta hydro-electric project, and this meant not frightening away capital by too socialist a policy. He knew that the CPP was not acceptable to all citizens. The traditionalists of the interior still regarded Nkrumah and his adherents as upstart 'verandah boys' from the coast.

In fact, Nkrumah had to win two more elections, those of 1954 and 1956, before independence. The least of his problems was convincing London. Before the 1956 election, the Conservative Colonial Secretary, Lennox-Boyd, promised that, if a 'reasonable majority' in the new legislature called for independence, he would set a date. The independence motion was passed by 72 votes to nil in a House of 104 members. Some would not vote for Nkrumah, although none would vote against independence.

Lennox-Boyd named 6 March 1957 as independence day. On attaining independence the new state took the name of Ghana. Ghana had been an ancient and rich African empire, which had flourished from about the fourth to the thirteenth centuries. It is a matter of dispute whether the inhabitants of modern Ghana are the direct descendants of ancient Ghanaians. But the choice of name is significant. The new Ghanaians wished to dissociate themselves from the whole colonial period and to return to something which they felt represented their real roots in the African continent. It was a precedent which was to be followed by other countries as they became independent.

The bright hopes which greeted Ghanaian independence soon faded. Nkrumah turned Ghana into a one-party state. Opposition leaders were arrested and J. B. Danquah died in prison. When Ghana became a republic under a new constitution in 1960, virtually dictatorial powers were conferred on Nkrumah as President. He continued to be an enthusiast for a Pan-African ideal of a united Africa; but in international terms he eschewed Nehru's non-alignment policies and, particularly after a visit to Russia and China in the summer of 1961, began to seek increasingly close links with the communist powers. He was deposed by an army coup in February

1966, while on a visit to Peking (Beijing). Ghana then alternated between brief attempts to restore civilian government and military rule. A new multi-party constitution was approved in 1992 but most opposition parties boycotted the subsequent elections. In 1996 Flt. Lt. Jerry Rawlings, who led the 1979 military coup, was re-elected President.

Although it was soon apparent that the Ghanaian experiment was not working out as expected the Conservative government in Britain was now committed to a full programme of decolonization in Africa. In February 1960 the Prime Minister, Harold Macmillan, made his famous 'wind of change' speech in Cape Town. (It was first made in Accra a few days earlier but not picked up by the world's press.) He told the South African Parliament:

> Ever since the break up of the Roman Empire one of the constant facts of political life in Europe has been the emergence of independent nations. . . . Fifteen years ago this movement spread through Asia. . . . Today the same thing is happening in Africa. . . . The wind of change is blowing through this continent, and whether we like it or not this growth of national consciousness is a political fact. We must all accept it as a fact and our national policies must take account of it. (Quoted in Madgwick et al., 1982, p. 286)

Nigeria

The first British colony in Africa to become independent after Macmillan's speech was Nigeria. Nigeria had looked to the British Colonial Office a less promising candidate for independence than Ghana. As a state it had to grow within entirely artificial boundaries, laid down mainly by the Royal Niger Company between 1885 and 1899. The Yorubas of the Western Region, the Ibos of the Eastern Region and the Moslem emirates of the North had little in common and sometimes heartily disliked one another. Lord Lugard, its most famous governor, had depended heavily on indirect rule which had worked well in the North, although confirming its essentially conservative character; less well in the South. Nigeria had not been particularly prosperous between the wars, and consequently there had been less spending on education and social services than in Ghana and the educated middle class was proportionately smaller. Nevertheless, nationalist sentiment had emerged in the inter-war period and, in particular, Nmandi Azikiwe on his return from America in 1935 had set up a chain of newspapers, including the *West African Pilot* and the *African Morning Post*, which had influenced opinion throughout British West Africa.

In Nigeria, as in the Gold Coast, the British government first tried 'constitution-mongering'. A new, very conservative, constitution, the Richards constitution (called after the Governor, Sir Arthur Richards), was introduced in 1946. Azikiwe, as the leader of a new political grouping, the National Council for Nigeria and the Cameroons, went to London to protest. The Richards constitution was replaced by the rather more liberal Macpherson constitution in 1951.

Three parties had now emerged. First, Azikiwe's NCNC, which tried to be an all-Nigerian party, but which was strongest in the Ibo Eastern Region. (Azikiwe was himself an Ibo, although born outside the Region.) Second, Chief Awolowo's Action Group in the Western Region. Third, the Northern People's Congress in the Northern Region, led by Ahmadu Bello, the Sardauna of Sokoto, with which Abubakar Tafawa Balewa was also associated.

Inspired by the progress being made in Ghana, the Nigerians began to demand early independence, and conferences were held in London and Lagos in 1953 and 1954. The British government was, however, seriously concerned about the security of religious and other minorities in Nigeria. A commission, which reported in 1958, was appointed 'to inquire into the fears of Minorities and the means allaying them'. The possibility of writing a kind of Bill of Rights into the constitution was also considered.

Yet another constitution came into force in 1954, this time frankly federalist. Significantly, in the 1954 elections all the main leaders, Azikiwe, Awolowo and the Sardauna, chose to stand for the House of Assembly in their own regions, rather than for the Federal House in Lagos. As a result Abubakar, not previously well known, became the most important leader in Lagos. Yet more constitutional conferences were held and independence was set for 1960.

Chief Awolowo, at least, was under no illusions about the difficulties facing his country. He had written in 1947, 'There is a popular illusion among educated young Nigerians about self-government. They believe that it is like "the Kingdom of God and his righteousness" which, once attained, brings unmixed blessing. They therefore seek it as a first objective. It is a clever way of evading the immediate problems which confront the country' (Awolowo, 1947, p. 30). He recognized the deep distrust that the illiterate majority had for the educated minority (ibid., p. 32). But the most intractable problem was the regional one. In what was probably a conscious echo of Metternich's judgement on Italy, he wrote, 'Nigeria is not a nation. It is a mere geographical expression' (ibid., p. 47). Studies of other countries with minority problems, Yugoslavia and the United Kingdom (he was interested in Scots and Welsh nationalism), did not reassure him, although he took some comfort from the successful experiment of Switzerland (ibid., pp. 50, 54).

The elections of December 1959 foreshadowed future problems. This time Azikiwe and Awolowo stood for the Federal House in Lagos. The Northern People's Congress, with its smaller ally, the Northern Elements Progressive Union, emerged as the strongest grouping with 150 seats, but without an overall majority. The NCNC won 89 seats; the Action Group, 73. Both the latter parties won some seats outside their own regions. But the Northern region had a big built-in advantage because it had been allocated 174 seats in a House of 320. This was resented in the South, which saw no chance of overcoming it, and contested the population statistics on which the allocation had been based.

After some political manoeuvrings, the NCNC agreed to serve under Abubakar in a coalition with the northern parties. Awolowo became leader of the opposition. Azikiwe did not take office but became Governor-General on independence on 1 October 1960 and President when the country became a republic in 1963.

In some ways the omens now seemed favourable. From being a poor country, Nigeria was becoming rich as the result of the discovery of oil and natural gas. But Nigeria was to collapse in even greater disarray than Ghana, from its own internal stresses. The Eastern Region increasingly resented what it saw as the domination of the North. Matters came to a head with the 1964 elections, when charges of blatant election-rigging were made at all levels.

In January 1966 the Eastern Region army staged a *coup d'état*. Abubakar, Ahmadu Bello and Akintola, a prominent Western Region politician favourable to the North, were assassinated. General Ironsi, an Ibo from the East, became president in place of Azikiwe, who had been absent in London, undergoing medical treatment at the time of the coup. But in July 1966 the Northern Region staged a counter-coup. Ironsi was assassinated and replaced by a Northerner, General Gowan. Gowan was not a typical Northerner. He was a Christian, not a Moslem, and from the south of the region; but any hope that he might prove a compromise candidate was destroyed by the widespread massacres of Ibos in the Northern Region. The survivors fled to their homeland in the Eastern Region.

The stage was set for the Nigerian civil war. On 30 May 1967 the Eastern Region proclaimed its secession as the independent republic of Biafra. The war went on for nearly three years, attracting worldwide attention, until the final defeat of the Biafrans and the flight of their leader, General Ojukwu, in January 1970. Nigeria remained under military government, while attempts were made to soften the stark divisions into three hostile regions by breaking the country up into 19 states in 1976. Civilian government was restored in 1979 but overthrown, after new allegations of corruption by another military coup in 1984. Subsequent attempts to restore civilian government have not so far (1999) been successful.

Sierra Leone and The Gambia

The other two British colonies in West Africa, Sierra Leone and The Gambia, may be dealt with briefly. Sierra Leone became independent on 27 April 1961. Dr Milton Margai's Sierra Leone People's Party won a large majority in the elections of 1962. There had always been tensions between the original colony, round the port of Freetown established as a home for freed slaves in the late eighteenth century, and the larger area of the Protectorate, acquired during the Scramble period. In March 1967 there was an army coup. Civilian government was subsequently restored, but Sierra Leone became officially a one-party state in 1978. Attempts were made to restore multi-party government and democracy in the early 1990s but the situation degenerated into civil war in 1997.

The Gambia presented a problem. Starting as a trading base on the River Gambia, it was the oldest British colony in West Africa; during the Scramble period it had become entirely surrounded, except for its narrow coastline, by the French territory of Senegal. It was scarcely viable economically, and various abortive attempts were made to exchange it with the French for territory elsewhere. By the mid-1880s, however, small size was no longer considered an automatic barrier to independent nation status and The Gambia became independent on 18 February 1965. In 1982, after Senegalese troops had helped to put down an attempted coup the previous year, The Gambia entered into a confederation with Senegal, although remaining an independent state. The confederation was dissolved in 1989.

East Africa (Uganda, Tanganyika and Zanzibar)

Those East African territories which had not attracted substantial European settlement, Uganda, Tanganyika and Zanzibar, were treated in much the same way as Britain's West African colonies although initially there were some doubts about that in the case of Uganda.

Uganda, although a rich and populous region, had often been turbulent. In the Scramble period European explorers and missionaries literally walked into problems and disturbances which they did not understand. Some of the tensions arose from the rivalries between the most powerful local kingdom, Buganda, under its Kabaka, and the smaller kingdoms of Bunvoro, Toro and Ankole. These old antagonisms, complicated now by other conflicts between colonial and indigenous interests, surfaced again in the years before independence when the young Kabaka, Mutesa II, opposed the British Governor, Sir Andrew Cohen, on behalf of the rights of the Baganda people. Cohen, a former head of the Africa Department of the Colonial Office, declared as soon as he arrived in Uganda in 1952 'the future of Uganda must lie in a unitary form of central Government on parliamentary lines covering the whole country' (quoted in Low, 1971, p. 105). Cohen was a sincere reformer and one of his first acts was to bring Africans into his Executive Council, but the Ugandans were suspicious that Cohen meant to force them against their will into an East African Federation with Kenya and Tanganyika, similar to the Central African Federation currently being formed (see p. 53). Mutesa determined to resist even the fusing of Buganda with the rest of Uganda. In November 1953 Cohen withdrew British recognition of Mutesa as Kabaka and deported Mutesa himself to London.

Mutesa's deportation caused a sensation and precipitated an important debate in the House of Commons on 2 December 1953 in which the Conservative Colonial Secretary, Oliver Lyttelton, was compelled to declare that Uganda's future was primarily as 'an African country'. An Australian academic, Sir Keith Hancock, then Director of the Institute of Commonwealth Studies in the University of London, was sent out as an independent expert to review the possibilities. Hancock's mission paved the way for the Namirembe conference of 1954 which defined the relations between Buganda and the rest of Uganda. The suggestion of an East African Federation was dropped, and with it ideas of 'partnership' between African, European and Asian communities in the region. Uganda was to be 'African'. Political parties began to form in the country but they remained exceptionally fragmented. No really powerful, concerted, nationalist party emerged (Low, 1971, p. 196).

With many problems unresolved, Uganda became independent on 9 October 1962. The following year the Kabaka became president, but relations between Buganda and the other three kingdoms making up the state of Uganda deteriorated. In 1966 Milton Obote, the Prime Minister, and subsequently 'Executive President', engineered a coup against the Kabaka, who fled to England. The man who led the troops against the Kabaka's palace in May 1966 was Idi Amin. In 1971, while Obote was abroad, Amin, now Army Commander, proclaimed himself Head of State and inaugurated one of the most blood-stained reigns in post-independence Africa. It took a military intervention from the neighbouring state of Tanzania in 1979 to overthrow him. Milton Obote returned as president in 1980 but was overthrown by a military coup in 1985.

Tanganyika differed from Uganda in that it was a former German colony mandated to Britain in 1919. Britain fulfilled her formal obligations to the League of Nations Mandate Commission but, in general, Tanganyika was assimilated to the norm of a British Crown Colony. As in neighbouring Uganda, the British relied a great deal upon the traditional authorities but in Tanganyika, unlike Uganda, a united nationalist movement began to emerge under Julius Nyerere, the son of a chief but also a typical 'first generation' nationalist, educated at Makerere and Edinburgh. After Tanganyika became independent on 9 December 1961, Nyerere's careful but firm handling of the economy gave Tanganyika over two decades of tranquility, rare in post-independence Africa.

In April 1964 Tanganyika united with the neighbouring state of Zanzibar. Zanzibar, consisting of the islands of Zanzibar, Pemba and Latham, had traditionally been the greatest trading centre of the East African coast. It had been British territory from 1890 until its independence in 1963. Its union with Tanganyika essentially restored its traditional relation with the hinterland, which had been severed when one became British and the other German during the Scramble period.

Kenya

Kenya presented the British government with a more severe test. Climatically it was suitable for European settlement and the British persuaded themselves in the late nineteenth century that it was full of wide-open, scarcely populated areas, a 'new Australia' in the enthusiastic phraseology of the time. They even briefly thought of it as a suitable 'National Home' for the Jews. British settlers went out in small numbers before and after the First World War, and in rather larger numbers after the Second, when some citizens became tired either of postwar austerity or of the policies of the Labour government. The British expatriate community in Kenya between the wars was the rackety one, well portrayed in James Fox's *White Mischief* (1982), but they introduced successful plantation farming of crops such as coffee and tea.

The British settlers had no doubt that the country belonged to them and expected to evolve a form of government like that of

Canada or Australia. They received a major setback in the Devonshire White Paper of 1923. (The Duke of Devonshire was Colonial Secretary in Bonar Law's government.) The White Paper told them bluntly that the grant of responsible government was 'out of the question' for the foreseeable future. It added: 'Primarily Kenya is an African territory, and His Majesty's Government think it necessary definitely to record their considered opinion that the interests of the African natives must be paramount, and that if and when those interests and the interests of the immigrant races should conflict the former should prevail.' In later years the British government did not always speak out so clearly but the essential principle remained.

The Devonshire White Paper had spoken of immigrant races in the plural, and the situation was further complicated by the existence of an Asian community which had come in, not as legend sometimes said, to build the railways but, more often, to take advantage of the railways to carry trade into the heart of the African continent. The Asians were prosperous and sometimes became money lenders. They were accordingly hated by the Africans in both Kenya and Uganda. In Kenya, inspired by the example of India, the Asians agitated for an extension of the franchise in the years after the First World War. A Legislative Council had been established in 1906, and in 1927 it was reconstructed so that it now comprised 20 official members, 11 elected Europeans, 5 elected Indians, 1 elected Arab and 1 nominated member to represent the Africans.

At this time the Africans had scarcely begun to organize themselves. Such organization as there was existed among the Kikuyu people. The Kikuyu had not previously been dominant in Kenya in the way in which the pastoral Masai had been, but they were farmers in the region where the capital, Nairobi, was established. They were more disturbed in the possession of their land than other tribes and they also came into contact with European ideas and European education. The later leader, Jomo Kenyatta, was first educated at a Presbyterian mission school. The first African organization, the Kikuyu Association, was formed in 1920; but it was a very moderate body, made up of the older men and the chiefs. In 1921 the Young Kikuyu Association (later the Kikuyu Central Association) was founded by the younger men, educated like Kenyatta himself in the mission schools, and was much more radical in temper.

Kenyatta was abroad from 1929 to 1946. When he returned he found that the Kikuyu Central Association had been condemned as seditious during the war and that very little constitutional progress seemed to have been made. Although by 1948 there was an unofficial majority in the Legislative Assembly, the four African members were still nominated. Only in 1952 were Africans elected to the Council and then by a complicated indirect system.

The early 1950s (1952–5) saw the terrorist outbreaks known as Mau Mau. They centred on the Kikuyu tribe and seem to have sprung from economic stresses and fears about land, rather than from political demands. With their fearsome oaths and occasional atrocities, they spread terror among the European community, although in fact most of the atrocities were committed against fellow Africans. Whether Kenyatta had any connection with Mau Mau has always been obscure but he was arrested and banished to a northern part of the colony.

The white colonists could not conquer Mau Mau on their own and had to ask for troop reinforcements from Britain. John Hatch is probably right in saying that this need to call on British troops finally ended any remaining pretensions that the settlers might have had that they would be capable of running an independent state (Hatch, 1965, p. 334).

In the midst of the Mau Mau troubles a new constitution was introduced into Kenya called the Lyttleton constitution after the British colonial secretary, Oliver Lyttleton. This was an extremely complicated system designed to allow the Africans to gain some ministerial experience. It was strongly opposed by the more diehard settlers; but Michael Blundell formed a new European party, the United Country Party, to work for a society which would be multiracial yet would safeguard both the political and land rights of the Europeans.

Even this was doomed. The tide was now firmly in favour of making Kenya an independent African country, although the Macleod constitution of 1960 (when Iain Macleod was colonial secretary) reserved some seats of the Legislative Council for various minority groups, including Europeans.

The Africans had now formed two main political parties; the Kenya African National Union (KANU), which drew its strength from the Kikuyu and Luo tribes and generally favoured a central-ized system of government, and the Kenya African Democratic Union (KADU), supported by the Masai and a number of smaller tribes, which would have preferred a more federal system of gov-ernment. KANU, led by Kenyatta, won the 1963 election, the last before independence on 12 December 1963.

Kenya under Kenyatta, like Tanzania under Nyerere, settled into a peaceful, albeit in practice a one-party, state. It became a one-party state officially in 1982, three years after Kenyatta's death. A multi-party system was introduced in 1992 but elections continued to be dominated by KANU.

South Central Africa (the Rhodesias and Nyasaland)

Rhodesia was to a peculiar degree the creation of one man, Cecil John Rhodes. In 1889, against considerable opposition, Rhodes obtained a Royal Charter for his British South African Company to enable him to open up the territory lying between the Transvaal and the Congo Free State, at first called Charterland and subse-quently Northern and Southern Rhodesia, the two provinces belng divided by the Zambesi river. The territory had previously been under the control of the Matabele chief, Lobengula, and, as the British Colonial Office soon realized, Rhodes's claims to have obtained jurisdiction as distinct from some economic concessions from Lobengula were suspect. But, with rival Portuguese and Ger-man claims in the area, the Colonial Office was inclined to let things ride. It was almost obsessed by the need to administer all these newly acquired territories cheaply, and so Company rule was al-lowed to continue in Southern Rhodesia until 1923 and in North-ern Rhodesia until 1924.

When the Company finally surrendered its political rights, North-ern Rhodesia reverted to being an ordinary crown colony; but the situation in Southern Rhodesia was more complicated. There was, by 1923, a considerable settler population there. These settlers had for some time been agitating against Company rule but, like the whites in Kenya, most of them looked to ultimate dominion status. There was an alternative possibility in 1923, and that was union with their southern neighbour, South Africa. Some Rhodesians favoured this, but it was defeated in a referendum. Instead, Southern Rhodesia became a 'self-governing colony'. The trouble was that this was a status not really known to constitutional law. It was not quite 'dominion status' (a well-understood concept by that time), although Rhodesian prime ministers attended the four-yearly `Imperial Conferences' and were treated as if they were dominion premiers. In theory, the British government retained some control over Rhodesian legislation and could veto any which was racially discriminatory. In fact, however, it did not exercise this right. The prejudice in favour of 'the local man knowing best' was very strong at this time and, in any case, race relations seemed tranquil in Rhodesia. Particularly after the Second World War, Rhodesia was held up to the world as an example of a country where a multiracial society was developing. This was over-optimistic but the situation was certainly better than in South Africa.

The white Rhodesians' belief that, between the wars, they had virtually enjoyed dominion status must be taken into account when assessing why they unilaterally declared their independence in 1965. In 1953, against the better judgement of some of them, they were persuaded by Britain to enter into a federation with Northern Rhodesia and Nyasaland. Economically this 'Central African Federation' made some sense. Southern Rhodesia was by now a very flourishing agricultural country (the gold which Rhodes and his associates had hoped to find there having proved illusory), while Northern Rhodesia had great mineral resources, particularly of copper. Nyasaland was regarded as too poor to be viable on its own. Its history was different from that of Rhodesia. Scottish Presbyterian missions had been active there in the nineteenth century – as a result it produced the best-educated young men in southern Africa, who were in demand over half the continent. It had become a British Protectorate in 1891.

The black population of the region were never in favour of the Federation. Serious labour and trade union troubles erupted in Northern Rhodesia where Kenneth Kaunda emerged as the significant figure. Kaunda, like Kenyatta, had been educated at mission schools. (His father, the Reverend David Kaunda, was a black Presbyterian minister). Rather unusually he had not been abroad for any part of his education.

The situation in Nyasaland approached the absurd. In March the European authorities declared a state of emergency, following a number of disturbances. They believed that there was a plot to massacre all the Europeans in the country. A British judge, Mr Justice (later Lord) Devlin, was sent out to investigate. The Devlin Report dismissed the 'massacre plot' as a chimera and severely criticized the authorities for over-reacting. Nyasaland too had now found its black leader in Dr Hastings Banda. He had returned home in July 1958, forty years after he had set out penniless to further his education, first in South Africa and subsequently in America and Scotland. He qualified as a doctor and spent many years in general practice in the United Kingdom.

When the Central African Federation was set up, provision had been made that it should be reviewed within ten years. In 1960 a Commission was sent out, under the chairmanship of Walter Monckton. It reported that each territory should have the right to secede. Three years of complicated negotiations ensued in which were involved, at various times, Iain Mcleod and Reginald Maudling, successively Colonial Secretaries, Duncan Sandys the Commonwealth Secretary (Southern Rhodesia still considered itself a dominion) and, most senior of all, R. A. Butler, who was given special responsibility for Central African Affairs. The Federation was dissolved on 31 December 1963. Nyasaland became independent as Malawi on 6 July 1964; Northern Rhodesia, as Zambia, on 24 October 1964.

The whites in Southern Rhodesia (or simply 'Rhodesia', as it was now generally called) felt that they had been betrayed and left stranded. If they had not entered the Federation, they argued, they would have had virtual independence. As it was, the climate of opinion had greatly changed and the British government was unwilling to accord formal independence until there was black majority rule. A new constitution had come into force in 1961 which gave the Africans 15 seats out of 65 in the Legislature and incorporated a 'Bill of Rights' for Africans. But the general thrust of Rhodesian policy was now going in the opposite direction. The whites were moving more and more towards South African attitudes, and the passage of the Law and Order Maintenance Bill in 1960 led to the resignation of the liberal Chief Justice, Sir Robert Tredgold.

An African nationalist movement had grown up in Rhodesia too. The founding father of black Rhodesian nationalism was Joshua Nkomo, but in 1963 his African National Congress split. Nkomo continued to lead the Zimbabwe African People's Union but a new and more radical group, the Zimbabwe African National Union was formed by the Reverend Ndabaningi Sithole. Zimbabwe was the name of the African empire which had once existed in the region, with its capital at Great Zimbabwe, the ruins of which exist to this day, and the reclaiming of the name Zimbabwe was parallel to the West African use of 'Ghana'. The split in the ranks of the nationalists helped the white Rhodesians to claim that black majority rule would lead to the kind of internecine strife which had devastated their neighbour Zaire (formerly the Belgian Congo) since its independence in 1960 (see p. 88).

On 11 November 1965 a white Rhodesian government led by Ian Smith issued its notorious Unilateral Declaration of Independence. Harold Wilson's Labour government in London was gravely embarrassed. Rejecting military intervention as impractical, the British relied upon economic sanctions to force the Rhodesians to surrender. In a phrase he was later to regret Wilson assured the world that sanctions would work in weeks rather than months. In fact sanctions proved almost totally ineffective, mainly because they were breached by Rhodesia's two neighbours, South Africa and Mozambique, the latter still a Portuguese colony at this time. It was the collapse of the Portuguese empire and South Africa's decision on political grounds not to continue to bolster the Rhodesian regime which, more than the increasingly intensive guerrilla warfare waged by the black nationalists, compelled the white Rhodesians to surrender in December 1979 and temporarily revert to the status of a British colony. Elections on the basis of universal suffrage were held in February 1980, and legal independence was granted on 18 April 1980.

The elections were ominous for the future because the electorate divided along clear tribal lines. Although the original split in 1963 had not been tribal in nature, the majority Shona-speaking people voted for ZANU, now led by Robert Mugabe; the minority Ndebele (Matabele) people in the south and west of the country continued to support Joshua Nkomo. Under Mugabe Zimbabwe became in practice a one-party state.

3

The British Empire: Outposts

The Caribbean

Most of the former British colonies in Africa, with the possible exception of The Gambia, were judged to be economically and politically viable as independent nation states. It was considered doubtful whether many of the British West Indian islands (with which for this purpose Bermuda and the Bahamas may be considered) were viable despite that fact that some of them, such as Jamaica, were old colonies with a long history of constitutional development. Various experiments were tried.

Parry and Sherlock (1971) identify three crucial decades in the history of the West Indies; the 'decade of freedom' in the 1830s when slaves were emancipated throughout the British empire; the 'decade of liberation' in the 1930s when people began to reject traditional attitudes, and the 'decade of independence' in the 1960s which saw the break-up of the British empire in the Caribbean (ibid., p. 299).

The changing attitudes of the 1930s were closely connected with economic crisis and the attempts of various groups to organize themselves to meet it. The price of sugar, the most important product of the British West Indies, fell catastrophically after 1929. The banana growers in Jamaica – bananas were Jamaica's principal export – also faced severe difficulties. The producers responded by forming co-operatives. The Banana Producers' Association was established in Jamaica in 1929. Similar groupings were formed by, among others, the nutmeg growers in Grenada and the citrus fruit growers in Trinidad and Jamaica. The primary producers thus considerably increased their bargaining power. Economic crisis also resulted in serious disturbances among the sugar workers and a few other groups between 1935 and 1938. For the first time trade unions became important in the islands. Trade unionism nurtured a number of important politicians, among them Norman Manley and W. A. (later Sir Alexander) Bustamente in Jamaica and Grantley Adams in Barbados. Combined with a growing sense of racial identity, fostered by men such as Marcus Garvey, the West Indians were beginning to develop a sense of both community and independence before the Second World War, which grew during the war, even though some of the economic problems eased.

The possibility of a federation of all the British West Indies, of which some people had dreamed for many years, came to seem a practical proposition in 1947 when a conference at Montego Bay voted in principle for a federation and set up a committee to draft a constitution. The draft was at last ready in 1953. It had been hoped that the two mainland territories of British Guiana and Honduras would join the federation. They declined for a variety of reasons, including a fear that they would be called upon to subsidize the poorer islands. Nevertheless the Federation came into being in 1958. It lasted barely three years. The islands were scattered over thousands of miles of sea. Particularist feelings in each island proved stronger than attachment to a rather nebulous Federation. The two largest islands, Jamaica and Trinidad, both relatively prosperous, came to resent the smaller islands as a drag upon them. In 1961 a referendum in Jamaica produced a majority in favour of secession. In August 1962 both Jamaica and Trinidad (with Tobago) became independent.

The problem of what to do with the smaller islands remained. Various forms of more limited federation were tried and abandoned. Barbados became independent in 1966; and in 1967 Antigua, Dominica, Grenada, St Kitts, Nevis, Anguilla and St Lucia (and a little later St Vincent) were linked with Britain as 'Associated States', which meant they had internal self-government but Britain remained responsible for defence and external affairs. However, even this was no longer regarded as satisfactory and, despite their extremely small size, all but one (Anguilla) have subsequently opted to become completely independent; Grenada in 1974, Dominica in 1978, St Lucia and St Vincent in 1979, Antigua in 1981 and St Kitts-Nevis in 1983. The hollowness of independent nation status for such small units was painfully demonstrated to the world by the American intervention in Grenada in the autumn of 1983 following the attempted coup which resulted in the murder of the prime minister, Maurice Bishop.

On the mainland, British Guiana became independent under the name of Guyana on 26 May 1966. The granting of independence to British Honduras (renamed Belize in 1973) was delayed by the insecurity engendered by the colony's long-standing dispute with neighbouring Guatemala. On more than one occasion the British Hondurans asked for the support of British troops. Nevertheless, independence was granted on 21 September 1981.

The Bahamas do not strictly speaking lie within the Caribbean but their road to independence was basically similar. Their prosperity began rather curiously between the wars when they provided a convenient base for boot-legging operations during American prohibition. It was boosted by their provision of facilities for air bases during the war. Postwar tourism has continued it. They became independent on 10 July 1973.

Bermuda gained internal self-government in 1968 but remains a British dependency. The Bermudans voted against independence in a referendum in 1995.

The Mediterranean

Britain acquired a number of Mediterranean possessions during her naval struggles with other European powers, principally France. Some, such as Minorca (returned to Spain in 1782), have long since ceased to be British.

Malta, taken from the French, who had taken it from the Knights of St John during the Napoleonic wars, was still an important British base in the Second World War. As Colin Cross (1968, p. 355) reminds us, the Maltese had always enjoyed a love-hate relationship with the British. In 1814 they had actually chosen to remain British. In 1955 the British government suggested that Malta should be treated as part of the United Kingdom, sending MPs to Westminster. This was entirely against the usual trend of British policy, which was always towards devolution not towards centralization at Westminster. Yet it only narrowly failed to gain acceptance, mainly because the British government was unwilling to undertake the expense of extending Britain's welfare state to Malta. In 1964 Malta became independent.

Cyprus was acquired on a lease from the Sultan of Turkey in 1878, at the time of the Congress of Berlin. It was meant to provide a forward naval base in the Eastern Mediterranean to guard the northern entrance to the Suez Canal opened in 1869. It proved useless as a naval base since it had no suitable deep water harbour, although it later became important as an air base. Its status was changed to that of a British colony when Turkey declared war on Britain in August 1914. It was one of the few possessions which Britain fought to retain after the Second World War.

In its way Cyprus provided Britain with as difficult a problem as Ireland, with clearly defined majority and minority populations who were hereditary enemies. The Greeks made up about 80 per cent of the population; the Turks about 20 per cent. The Greek population wanted *enosis*, union with Greece. In 1950 Michael Mouskos, the Bishop of Kitium, was elected Archbishop of Cyprus and took the title of Makarios III. He supplied the *enosis* movement with extremely astute political leadership. In 1956 the British exiled him to the Seychelles but his influence remained. In Cyprus itself Colonel Grivas, a Cypriot who had served with the Greek army, only intensified his guerrilla campaign. The British poured more and more troops into Cyprus, hoping to defeat Grivas as Templer had defeated the communist guerrillas in Malaya, but the situation was totally different. The majority of the Cypriot population were with Grivas. In July 1954 a Colonial Office minister had rashly said that Cyprus could never expect to be independent. But the British prime minister, Harold Macmillan, was a man who knew when he was beaten. Although it cost him the resignation of Lord Salisbury from his government, he ordered the release of Makarios in March 1957. After further negotiations with the governments of Greece and Turkey as well as with the Cypriots, Cyprus became independent in August 1960.

Salisbury's resignation marked an important turning-point in British imperial policy. Like Churchill he had firmly opposed the dissolution of the empire. Salisbury was at that time regarded as the 'king-maker' in the Conservative party, and it was generally believed to have been his influence which had ensured that Harold Macmillan, rather than R. A. Butler, had succeeded Anthony Eden as Prime Minister a few months earlier. But Salisbury's resignation attracted little support. 'The empire in danger' was no longer a rallying cry, even in the Conservative party.

The British public had been disillusioned by the fiasco of the Suez intervention the previous year. In 1882 British forces had occupied Egypt, mainly to safeguard the Suez Canal which was vital for communications with Britain's Indian empire. Gladstone's government had insisted that this was a mere 'police operation' and that the army would be withdrawn as soon as order was re-stored. The withdrawal was delayed, first by the Mahdi's cam-paign in the Sudan and subsequently by the fear that, if Britain moved out, some other great power might move in. Britain did not regularize her position in Egypt in terms of international law until the First World War, when Egypt became a British Protectorate. The Protectorate was formally terminated in 1922, but Britain re-tained very considerable powers of intervention, particularly to provide for the defence of Egypt. Only in March 1956 were all British troops withdrawn from the country. The Sudan had become independent earlier the same year.

In July 1956 the Egyptian president, Colonel Nasser, announced the nationalization of the Suez Canal. Both Britain and France were hostile to the move but it was difficult to contend that it was ille-gal, at least so long as Egypt observed the 1888 Convention per-mitting the ships of all nations to pass through the canal. In fact the Egyptians had prevented Israeli cargoes passing through since 1948 on the grounds that, in common with other Arab countries, they did not recognize Israel as a national state. After various attempts at international mediation had failed, Britain and France launched a military action in November 1956, nominally to prevent an Is-raeli–Egyptian clash, in fact in collusion with Israel. The British prime minister, Anthony Eden, was influenced by his memories of 'appeasement' in the 1930s and haunted by the thought that Hitler should have been checked much earlier in his aggressive career. But the rest of the world did not see Nasser as a new Hitler. British opinion was deeply divided. Both the superpowers, Russia and the United States, made it clear that they regarded the Anglo-French action as intolerable. In December the Anglo-French force was withdrawn with nothing accomplished.

It was doubly ironic that Britain should have gone into the Suez adventure as Israel's ally. In 1919 she had become the mandatory power for Palestine. Two years earlier the British Foreign Secretary, Arthur Balfour, had issued the famous Declaration:

> His Majesty's Government view with favour the establishment in Palestine of a national home for the Jewish people, and will use their best endeavours to facilitate this object, it being clearly understood that nothing shall he done which may prejudice the civil and religious rights of the existing non-Jewish communities in Palestine.

This was, of course, impossible. The land to be given to the Jews was already occupied by the Palestinians. For the next thirty years Britain had to live with the consequences of the Balfour Declaration. Between the wars the British tried, not always with success, to allow only a controlled flow of Jewish immigrants to come into the country. The pressure was inevitably much greater after the Second World War. The Jews who had survived Hitler's persecutions, joined by increasing numbers from elsewhere, were determined to set up a Jewish state in Palestine. The British still tried to keep the floodgates half-closed. The blowing-up of the King David Hotel in Jerusalem by a Jewish terrorist group, the Irgun, with many civilian casualties deeply shocked a British public less hardened to terrorism than it came to be a generation later. But more influential than terrorism was the American attitude. The American government, not unaware of electoral considerations – for the Jewish vote was vital in some key states such as New York – sympathized with Jewish aspirations. American attitudes played some part in persuading the British to leave India; they played more in persuading them to leave Palestine. The British announced that they would go, come what might, in June 1948. The boundaries of Israel remain unsettled even after a series of wars with her neighbours.

The 'Daughters'

In 1829 the radical *Westminster Review*, pursuing one of its fa-
vourite themes that 'it is pretty much with colonies as with children', opined that the sons would naturally go out into the world
on their own account and that the parting must, if possible, be ami-
cable, but that there would be some 'sickly infants' and 'unmarried daughters' who must remain at home. If the ghost of that leader
writer had returned to the world towards the end of the twentieth
century he might still have felt his analysis correct.

In the 1990s Britain was left with a few colonies, mainly islands, too small by any standards to become independent nations.
In some cases opponents of British policy might contend that they
were still 'unmarried daughters' because Britain had declined to
give their obvious spouses. Spain had long felt that it had a prior
claim to Gibraltar; but the Gibraltarians had expressed, through a
referendum, a determination to remain British. It would have been
difficult for Britain to have handed Gibraltar to General Franco's
fascist government, particularly after the Second World War, in
which Franco had heen generally regarded as Hitler's ally. When
Franco died, positions had been too long held to be easily abandoned.

The Falkland Islands are in a somewhat similar position. Acquired because they were thought, wrongly, to command the route
round Cape Horn, they had come to be regarded as an anachro-
nism by the 1970s. The Foreign Office view was that they must
ultimately be transferred to Argentina, upon which they were already heavily dependent for services. Unfortunately, such a transfer when Argentina itself was under the control of an extreme
right-wing military regime, was politically and morally impossible. General Galtieri's attempt to seize the islands by force in 1982
has ruled such a transfer out of court for the foreseeable future.

Hong Kong, acquired in 1842 at the end of the opium war, was
in a different position, in that the 'Mainland Territories' leased
from China in 1898, without which the island of Hong Kong is not
viable, were in any case due to return to China in 1997. It was
clear that the retention of Hong Kong by force was not a practical

proposition and, in 1984, the British government negotiated with Beijing the terms upon which the whole settlement was to be returned to China. Hong Kong was to be 'a special administrative region', still enjoying some distinctive identity. It suited China well enough to keep Hong Kong as a great international port with a special status, particularly an economic one, and on this basis Hong Kong was handed over in a formal ceremony on 1 July 1997. Some have seen this symbolic act as marking the final end of the British empire, the empire upon which in its heyday 'the sun never set'.

In fact a few British possessions remain, among them Anguilla, Montserrat, Ascension Island, St Helena, the Caymen Islands and the British Virgin Islands. A more important legacy is the Commonwealth.

4

The Commonwealth

In December 1946 Winston Churchill rounded on Prime Minister Clement Attlee in the House of Commons. He thundered:

> It was said, in the days of the great Administration of Lord Chatham, that one had to get up very early in the morning in order not to miss some of the gains and accessions of territory which were then characteristic of our fortune. The no less memorable Administration of the Right Hon. Gentleman opposite is distinguished for the opposite set of experiences. The British Empire seems to be running off almost as fast as the American Loan. (Quoted in Bennett, 1962, p. 422)

But most of the newly independent nations chose to remain members of the British Commonwealth of Nations. The decision of both India and Pakistan to remain members in 1947 caused some surprise, as well as gratification, in London. Discounting some mandated territories, the only important exceptions were Burma, Sudan and Aden (the last became part of the People's Republic of South Yemen in 1967).

The question of whether to stay in the Commonwealth had divided Indian nationalists in the 1920s and 1930s. On the whole the first generation of African nationalists had regarded it as desirable (see, for example, Awolowo, 1947, pp. 27–9). The question was whether the 'White Man's Club' of 1931 could broaden into a multiracial international grouping.

The inter-war period was the heyday of dominion status. The classic definition of the relationship between Britain and her then dominions, Canada, Australia, New Zealand and South Africa, was provided by the Balfour Declaration of 1926 which stated:

> They are autonomous Communities within the British Empire, equal in status, in no way subordinate one to another in respect of their domestic or external affairs, though united by a common allegiance to the Crown, and freely associated as members of the British Commonwealth of Nations. (Quoted in Keith, 1961, p. 161)

This was given legal substance by the Statute of Westminster of 1931. The problem was that, as the Balfour Report itself recognized, cohesion between these geographically scattered countries ultimately depended on a common heritage and a common outlook.

One problem was that the Balfour Report had defined members of the Commonwealth as being 'united by a common allegiance to the Crown'. The implication seemed to be that a republic could not be a member. Technically, that was the ground upon which Ireland left the Commonwealth when it declared itself a republic in 1949 (Mansergh, 1958, pp. 265–304). But by this time other countries, notably India and Pakistan, wished to become republics but also wished to stay in the Commonwealth. A formula was found in April 1949 which merely described the king (George VI) as the 'the Head of the Commonwealth' and the Crown as the 'symbol of the free association of its independent member states'. This was deemed to be quite compatible with India becoming a republic in 1950. By the 1960s it was regarded as normal for a former colony to become a republic, if not immediately, certainly within a few years of becoming independent. A convention had, however, grown up that a state on becoming a republic should seek the approval of other Commonwealth countries for its continued membership. When the Union of South Africa, already under strong international attack for its apartheid policies and its treatment of the former mandated territory of Namibia (German South West Africa), became a republic in 1961 it chose not to seek continued membership. Its defection was a relief to other Commonwealth countries, and especially to Britain, which wished to be no longer held in any way responsible for South Africa's position.

The first Colonial Conference was held in 1887. It was a more or less informal gathering of various colonial statesmen who happened to be in London for Queen Victoria's golden jubilee. The next was not held until 1897 on the occasion of Victoria's diamond jubilee. From 1907 the Conference became a regular four-yearly meeting attended by the prime ministers of the dominions. Other ministers, especially finance ministers, also met fairly frequently. Schemes for imperial federation, briefly popular in late Victorian times, had foundered on the diversity and scattered nature of the empire but a satisfactory degree of co-operation seemed to have been attained.

Many doubted whether these arrangements would survive the Second World War and the period of rapid decolonization. The central administration of the empire in London changed rapidly. The Colonial Office was abolished in 1967. The Dominions Office became the Commonwealth Relations Office in 1947 and finally merged with the Foreign Office in 1969.

Two questions strained the continuation of the Commonwealth. The first was the question of common citizenship. This had caused few problems in Queen Victoria's day. Apart from some 'protected persons' in British protectorates, all were subjects of the queen and, as a consequence, could move freely from one part of the empire to another. The Australians imposed restrictions on Asian immigration before the First World War and caused embarrassment at Colonial Conferences as a result. As the dominions became more conscious of their own nationhood between the wars, they began to define their citizenship more closely. United Kingdom citizenship was only defined in 1948 and no barriers to the entry of other Commonwealth citizens were erected until 1962. But each member nation of the Commonwealth now tends to treat citizens of other member nations very much like any other foreign nationals.

The second problem arose from the development of other international groupings which could sometimes conflict with the idea of a primary loyalty to the Commonwealth. All members were also members of the United Nations. Some Commonwealth members joined the Afro-Asian bloc formed at Bandung in 1955; others joined the Organization of African Unity, established at Addis

Ababa in 1963. Britain herself became a member of the North Atlantic Treaty Organization in 1949, a defensive alliance which included only one other Commonwealth country, Canada. More
importantly, in 1973, Britain, after many years of hesitation and
rebuffs, joined the European Economic Community. Although she
negotiated some concessions for her former Commonwealth trading partners (as the French had done for members of the French
Community) it was clear that Britain's primary economic commitment was now to Europe.

But, as a rather surprised headline in the *Observer* newspaper
commented in 1969, 'The Commonwealth survives obituaries'.
Regular meetings of Commonwealth heads of government continue to be held; indeed they are now held more frequently, every
two years instead of the traditional four. There are also annual
meetings of finance ministers and *ad hoc* meetings of other ministers. The Commonwealth Secretariat, established in 1965, coordi-
nates activities. The Commonwealth also acts as an umbrella for a
large number of non-governmental organizations, sporting, cultural and educational.

The Commonwealth formally ceased to be designated 'the British Commonwealth' in 1965. The Commonwealth prime ministers
met for the first time outside London, in Lagos, in 1966. This was
a special meeting to discuss the Rhodesian crisis but the regular
biennial meetings now rarely meet in the United Kingdom. How
little the Commonwealth was now regarded as being specifically
'British' was illustrated by the fact that in 1965 two countries, Ghana
and Tanzania, temporarily broke off diplomatic relations with Britain, because of what they regarded as her unsatisfactory response
to the Rhodesian situation, but did not feel obliged to leave the
Commonwealth.

The Commonwealth has assumed a moral authority in scrutiniz-
ing its members' conduct much more vigorous than that of the
United Nations. South Africa left in 1961 because it knew it would
be voted out. It returned amidst considerable rejoicing in 1994 when
apartheid had been abolished and majority rule established. Fiji
was forced out in 1987 after the elected government was overthrown by a *coup d'état* but reinstated in 1997. Nigeria was suspended in 1995 because of its disregard of human rights. The

Commonwealth formally established its standards of democracy, the rule of law, good government and social justice in Harare in 1991 and made them the basis for membership at the Cyprus meeting in 1993. Occasionally members have left, at least temporarily for other reasons. Pakistan (the former East Pakistan) left in 1972 in protest at the decision of other members to recognize West Pakistan as the independent state of Bangladesh. It returned in 1989. Even more surprisingly, Mozambique, which had never been a British colony, successfully applied to join in 1995. The Commonwealth now includes 54 member states, 33 of which are republics.

5

The French Empire

By the twentieth century the British empire was by far the largest of the European maritime empires, embracing, as its admirers were prone to say, one quarter of the world's population. The next biggest was the French empire, centred mainly on Africa. At its greatest extent it controlled one third of the African continent, even though some of that was the Sahara desert – 'very light soil, I believe', as the British prime minister, Lord Salisbury, once remarked. The other centre of gravity of the French empire was Indochina.

The French had lost most of their first empire, in Canada and in India, to the British in the eighteenth century, although remnants of that older empire survived, for example in the West Indies. They had acquired their second empire mostly after 1871. The spur had partly been defeat in the Franco-Prussian war. There was always conflict in French policy between those who saw France's real destiny and greatness lying in Europe and overseas adventures as a dangerous distraction, and those who felt that France must be a world power in order to establish her great-power status beyond question. Despite the complaints of those who saw the colonists as playing Bismarck's game for him, the French empire steadily expanded in the age of the new imperialism. Defeat in another war in 1940 was eventually to be fatal to the maintenance of this French empire even though, unlike the British, the French were, after the Second World War, prepared to fight to keep their empire.

This reflected the quite different thrust of French imperial policy. In fact, in the early twentieth century the French did not officially refer to their 'empire' (Gifford and Louis, 1971, p. 544). This was partly because a term reminiscent of the Bonapartes did not appeal to good republicans. But significantly the French preferred the title *La France d'outre-mer* – 'France overseas'. However much it might be impressed upon French colonial administrators that conditions varied, even between one African colony and another, the ideal of assimilation was not dead (ibid., pp. 545–6). The 'civilizing mission' had a reality in French politics and deep roots in French eighteenth-century philosophy. When Montesquieu, Voltaire, Rousseau or Diderot set out to establish the laws which should govern human society, they believed that they were discovering universal laws, comparable to the laws of physics which governed the whole world of nature, and which would apply to all societies. They did not envisage different laws for Frenchmen, Germans, Senegalese or Chinese. As a result, the French felt fewer inhibitions about changing other people's cultures or administration than did the British, even when for reasons of practical politics the French had to adopt something not unlike 'indirect rule'. Chiefs might be retained but they tended to be renamed 'sub-administrators'.

The brief experiment of the Second Republic of 1848–52 meant that full French citizenship was conferred on the inhabitants of the 'Anciennes Colonies': Martinique, Guadeloupe, Réunion, the old colony of Senegal and a few other small territories. They were allowed to send deputies to Paris. This last privilege was withdrawn under the Second Empire but restored in September 1870. Under the Third Republic the representation of the French colonies in the Senate and the Chamber of Deputies was somewhat haphazard. Whether a colony had representation, how many representatives there were and how they were selected varied according to historical circumstances. Their presence in the Chambers, particularly in an era of minority governments and wafer-thin majorities, was sometimes resented. On one occasion a representative from Cochin-China brought down a cabinet on a question concerning the mayoralty of Paris (Roberts, 1963, p. 79). These deputies were, however, for the most part Frenchmen who happened to be resident in the colonies, with some admixture of Creoles (those of mixed blood). Blaise Diagne was the first black African elected to represent Senegal, and that was as late as 1914 (July, 1968, pp. 392–404).

Economically, as well as politically, the organization of the French empire had traditionally been much tighter than that of the British. The full rigour of the *Pacte Colonial*, by which France had controlled the minutiae of her colonies' trade, was ended in 1868; but protective tariffs were restored in the 1880s and the Méline tariff, introduced in 1892, lasted until the Second World War.

In 1940 France made peace with Adolf Hitler's Germany. Part of France, including Paris, remained under German occupation and a French government was installed at Vichy. The defeat of France inevitably had the same kind of psychological impact throughout the French colonies as the defeat of Spain by France during the Napoleonic wars had had on Spain's American empire. The prestige of the mother country had disintegrated like Humpty Dumpty and could never really be put together again. But there were further complications for the French empire during the Second World War. Those who were still fighting Hitler did not recognize the legitimacy of the Vichy government's jurisdiction over the French colonies. General de Gaulle secured French Equatorial Africa for the Free French. For a time Vichy controlled French North and West Africa and Madagascar; but North Africa soon became a battleground between the British (later joined by the Americans) and the Germans. In 1942–3 the Anglo-American forces drove Germany and her allies out of North Africa. On the other side of the world, as the result of an agreement between Vichy and Tokyo, French Indochina was occupied by the Japanese from 1941 to 1945.

In 1946 the Fourth French Republic replaced the Third. The new constitution embodied what it was hoped would be a new deal for France's overseas empire. Metropolitan France, the existing *Départements d'Outre-Mer* (Algeria, the Caribbean colonies, St Pierre et Miquelon and Réunion) and the existing *Territoires d'Outre-Mer* (West and Equatorial Africa, Madagascar and the Pacific Islands) would form the French Union. Those countries which were too distinctive to be fitted into the Union, Indochina and the 'protected states' of Morocco and Tunis, became 'Associated States', with internal autonomy but with France still exercising control over their foreign policy.

All the inhabitants of the Union became French citizens with equal civil rights. This abolished the distinction between *citoyens* (citizens) and *sujets* (subjects) in the overseas territories. Previously the latter had not only not enjoyed full civil rights but were sometimes liable to especial burdens such as the obligation to perform labour services.

The French Union endured, despite many strains, until 1958. In that year de Gaulle returned to power and the Fourth Republic was superseded by the Fifth. The constitutional changes again involved the empire overseas. The French Union was replaced by the French Community, which was a much looser form of organization although it was still intended that foreign, defence and economic policy should be determined collectively. Each overseas territory was given the chance to hold a referendum to determine whether it wished to remain in the Community. All except Guinea voted to do so. But the Community, like the Union, was soon to be overtaken by changing circumstances and changing attitudes.

North Africa

Algeria was unique in the French empire in that it alone had attracted any significant amount of French settlement. France had first become involved with Algeria in 1830 when the last Bourbon king, Charles X, had mounted an expedition to flush out the Barbary pirates who still preyed on shipping in the Mediterranean. The French soon found that it was easier to get into, than to get out of, such involvement. In the 1830s and 1840s they were drawn into the conquest of the whole of Algeria, despite the strenuous resistance of Arab nationalist leaders, such as Abd-el-Kader. Napoleon III was attracted by the idea of 'military colonists' (time-expired soldiers) on the Roman pattern to provide a French presence in Algeria, and the first French settlers were encouraged to make their homes there. French policy towards Algeria was never consistent, least of all in the treatment of the majority population, the Arabs; but, more than any other area, it was increasingly treated as genuinely a *département* of metropolitan France.

This made ultimate decolonization all the more difficult. Arab resistance had never entirely ceased. After the Second World War it became much more active. France had lost control of the region altogether during the war and, whatever they might be promised under the French Union, the nationalists were not happy to see the restoration of a situation in which economic and political dominance remained with the settlers, who made up only about one-sixth of the population. Arab nationalism was powerfully reinforced by the general resurgence of Islam, which had been apparent to some perceptive men even in the nineteenth century but which gathered momentum in the twentieth.

The first serious rising took place on 1 November 1954, when some previously divided nationalist groups came together to form the National Liberation Front (FLN), and called on their fellow Algerians to rise. The Algerians were cautious and no mass rising immediately followed, but the French were never able to extinguish the FLN. Before the Algerian war ended, half a million French troops had been committed there. Their failure to solve the Algerian problem was a major factor in bringing down the Fourth Republic.

Initially, General de Gaulle had no greater success, although his management of public relations was a great deal better than that of his predecessors. But Algeria was now becoming a matter of international concern. Other Arab countries were expressing their support for the FLN. Another danger also loomed. Many of the French settlers were determined not to be sold out, as they saw it, by the French government. In January 1960 the barricades went up in Algiers, manned not by the nationalists but by the settlers. Some French army officers now took a hand and formed the Secret Army Organization (OAS) to oppose any transfer of power. De Gaulle's own life was in real danger, but he pressed on to achieve the Evian settlement with the Algerian nationalists between May 1961 and March 1962. Agreement was reached on 18 March and the proposed settlement put to a referendum in France on 8 April. De Gaulle's prestige – and a great weariness about the continuing war in Algeria – carried the day. Over 90 per cent voted in favour. A referendum in Algeria in July gave an almost 100 per cent majority.

Algeria became independent on 3 July 1962. French settlers in Algeria fared less well than did British settlers in Kenya or Rhodesia. In 1963 all agricultural land held by foreigners was expropriated, and by 1965 over 80 per cent of the settlers had left.

There were some French settlers in Tunis and Morocco, but these countries represented a minor problem compared with Algeria. Constitutionally, relations with France were also very different. Both Tunis and Morocco were 'Protected States' with their internal organization left largely intact. There was some violence in the early 1950s, and in Morocco the situation was complicated by conflicts between the supporters and opponents of the sultan. Complete independence was granted to Morocco on 2 March 1956 and to Tunis on 20 March. Both Tunis and Morocco were prepared to sign treaties continuing economic and other ties with France.

Black Africa and Madagascar

Just as the British were able to maintain links with their former colonies through the Commonwealth, so the French retained ties through the French Community. This was particularly true in Black Africa where the emergent states were often too weak, both politically and economically, to sustain their independence with any great confidence. French intervention in her former empire has, in fact, usually been a good deal more open than that of Britain.

At the outbreak of the Second World War France administered most of her African colonies in two large groups: French West Africa included Mauretania, Senegal, Guinea, the Ivory Coast, Dahomey, French Sudan, French Guinea, Upper Volta and Niger; French Equatorial Africa included Chad, Gabon, Middle Congo and Ubanghi-Shari. The mandated territories of Togoland and Cameroun were administered separately. When independence came these large units mostly separated out again into their component parts.

With a few exceptions, the struggle here was political rather than military. Even before the Second World War the Popular Front government in France after 1936 had made tentative moves towards associating the inhabitants of these colonies more closely with the government in Paris. During the war, first Equatorial and later West Africa became a base for the Free French and so were familiarized wilh the allied wartime propaganda on the right of self-determination for all peoples. The Brazzaville Conference of

January–February 1944 at which de Gaulle himself was present, although it was summoned avowedly to answer mainly American criticisms about continued colonialism, concerned itself not with decolonization, as this term later came to be understood, but with a new and improved programme of assimilation (Gifford and Louis, 1982, pp. 143–4,190–3). It was this (although not quite in the form de Gaulle himself would have preferred) which took shape in the French Union in 1946.

The year 1960 was the year of wonders in French, as in British, decolonization in Black Africa. The impetus came as much from Paris as from the colonies. Only two years earlier all the states involved, except Guinea, had seemed happy to remain in the French Community on the terms then on offer. But the French public was disillusioned by the war in Algeria, then going very badly, and the war in Indochina, already lost. The way had been opened by the *loi cadre* (outline law) of 1956, which provided for a considerable extension of representative government in each of the territories, although at that time it had been supposed that this would be within a continuing federal structure. Black African leaders like the veteran Senegalese, Leopold Senghor, at that time a deputy in Paris, were associated with the drafting of the *loi cadre*. The transfer of power came quickly in 1960 – to Cameroun in January, to Togo in April, to Mali in June, to the Ivory Coast, Dahomey (Benin), Upper Volta, Niger, Chad, Gabon, Middle Congo (People's Republic of Congo) and Ubanghi-Shari (Central African Republic) in August, and to Mauretania and Senegal (after it had split from Mali) in November. Even those states which did not opt to stay formally within the French Community chose to retain many economic, financial and technological links with France. It was not quite the preferred French solution of Union (although that had in fact attracted criticism in metropolitan France from those who did not like the prospect of a solid phalanx of colonial deputies in the Chambers); but it seemd to be the next best thing, a smooth transfer of power to *évolués*, westernized men who had absorbed a great deal of French culture and values, and who could be expected to continue to cooperate with France. In fact the very closeness of the association could itself be a cause of embarrassment, as when the dealings between Colonel Bokassa (the self-styled emperor of the

Central African Republic) and president Giscard d'Estaing in the late 1970s helped to discredit the President and his party before the French presidential elections of 1981.

The transfer of power was less smooth in Madagascar. The island had nominally been a French protectorate since 1885; but the French had had to fight hard in the 1890s to overthrow the Hova dynasty and to conquer what, despite its racially diverse population drawn partly from Africa and partly from Asia, was an organized and viable state. A serious rising broke out in 1929. When the Free French forces took control of the island in 1942 the Madagascans, more than most, looked to the promises in the Atlantic Charter as a guarantee of future independence, although possibly still in association with France. They were bitterly disillusioned after the war by French procrastination and the tenderness shown to the interests of the French settlers on the island. There was a new rising in March 1947, which was suppressed with particular brutality by a very frightened colonial government. The Madagascans voted to stay in the French Community in 1958 but the movement for independence was already strong. In 1959 they elected their own President and became formally independent as the Malagasy Republic in June 1960.

Indochina

In some ways the French empire in Indochina resembled that of the British in India, although it lasted a very much shorter time. Both empires were established in the midst of an ancient and sophisticated culture, with great social cohesion despite the political disarray. The relationship between Indochina and its vast northern neighbour, China, was a complex one. For a thousand years, until about AD 900, Vietnam had actually been the southernmost province of the Chinese empire and China had made a number of subsequent attempts to reconquer it. Although these had not succeeded Vietnam, like its two neighbours, Laos and Cambodia, continued to pay tribute to China and to acknowledge some kind of feudal overlordship.

Vietnam's official relations with France began in 1787, in the reign of Louis XVI, when the two countries concluded a commercial treaty; but it was not until 1859 that Napoleon III, taking advantage of some alleged persecution of French Roman Catholic missionaries, seized control of Saigon, which he hoped to make into a port which would rival Singapore. During the next decade France annexed the southernmost part of Vietnam, Cochin-China. But only after the Third Republic came into power in France after the Franco-Prussian war did the French go on to conquer the rest of Vietnam. In 1884 the treaty of Hué regulated the French protectorate over Annam and Cambodia and the treaty was reluctantly recognized by China in the following year. The French had the greatest difficulty in 'pacifying' the northernmost Vietnamese province of Tonkin, with its ancient capital of Hanoi. They battled for years against the 'pirates' or 'black flags', some of them Chinese irregulars, some refugees from the Taiping rebellion in China. The skirmishes brought down one French government, that of Jules Ferry in 1885, in spectacular circumstances (the mob converged on the Chamber of Deputies, demanding that the prime minister be hanged from the nearest lamp post). The protectorate of Laos was acquired rather more peacefully when Thailand ceded the province in 1893.

The Vietnamese already had a sense of nationhood, of the *quoc* or country, forged in their struggles with China (Smith, 1968, pp. 40–2), although it had not always been reflected in coherent political organization. In 1802, however, Nguyên Anh united the whole of Vietnam and ruled as the emperor, Gia-Long. It was his descendent, Tu-Duc, who was compelled to come to an accommodation with the French in the 1880s.

The Indochinese, like the Indians, differed among themselves in their reactions to European culture. The French recognized that here assimilation was scarcely practical and emphasized rather association. Nevertheless, some Vietnamese embraced western ideas. A significant minority abandoned the traditional creeds of Confucianism, Buddhism and Taoism in favour of Roman Catholicism. Quite a number of young men went to Paris for an education.

Political opposition to the French was from the beginning organized and sophisticated. Vietnamese nationalists were interested in the developments in Japan and, until prevented by the French in 1909, keen to go and study there. They were also influenced by the growing opposition to the British in India and still more by the Chinese nationalist revolution of Sun Yat-sen in 1911. In 1904 a group of young scholars formed the *Duy-Tân Hôi* (Reform Association) to work for an independent Vietnam and a reformed monarchy. Four years later a peasant revolt broke out in central Vietnam and although it was probably mainly directed against immediate grievances such as high taxation and forced labour, it had some connection with the *Duy-Tân Hôi* and provided the French with an excuse for repressive measures. The movement which most closely resembled the Indian National Congress was the *Parti Constitutionaliste*, formed in Saigon in 1917, among French-educated Vietnamese. They asked, among other things, for an expansion of education and the creation of a representative council or parliament in Vietnam. This last was a dangerous demand and quite against the trend of official French thinking, and they gave the *Parti Constitutionaliste* none of the official recognition accorded to the Indian National Congress by the British. Disillusioned, a number of young nationalists began to move towards communism, which was already establishing itself in China in the inter-war period (Smith, 1968, pp. 86–97).

The most important convert was Nguyen Ai Quoc (Nguyen the Patriot), better known to history as Ho Chi Minh. The son of a mandarin family, he had sailed to France as a cabin boy on a steamer in 1912. In 1919 he presented a petition to the Paris Peace Conference, asking for Vietnamese independence. When this was ignored he turned to communism and helped to found the modern French Communist Party at Tours in 1920. In 1923 he went to Moscow and subsequently to China. From Canton he organized a revolutionary group in Vietnam, the *Thanh-Niên Hôi*. The years 1930–1 saw a number of revolts in various parts of Vietnam, of which those led by the *Thanh-Niên Hôi* were the most effective.

The story of decolonization in Indochina differs from that of any other part of the old European empires in that, although it had its origins in local nationalism, it became an open confrontation between the communist and the non-communist world. The peculiarity of the Indochinese situation arose partly from the events of the Second World War and partly from the triumph of communism in China in 1949.

Indochina was a rich area. In 1923 Albert Sarraut called it 'the most prosperous of all our colonies' (Sarraut, 1923, p. 463). By 1939, although rice was still the staple crop, rubber, sugar-cane, cotton and coffee were being produced for export. Vietnam had both iron and coal and there was a significant textile industry. Its economic wealth and its strategic position led the Japanese to demand that it be placed under their control in 1941.

In 1941 the Vietminh Front was organized in southern China. Its secretary was Ho Chi Minh (he adopted that name in 1942) and the communists were the backbone of the movement, although it was an umbrella organization for a number of groups and its avowed aim was simply the liberation of Vietnam. In August 1945, after the Japanese surrender, the Vietminh seized control of Hanoi and secured the abdication of the emperor, Bao-Dai. On 2 September Ho Chi Minh read the 'Declaration of Independence of the Democratic Republic of Viet-Nam'. It began with Thomas Jefferson's words, `We hold these truths to be self-evident. That all men are created equal.' American army officers stood by approvingly (Herring, 1979, p. 1).

Until the Yalta Conference in February 1945, the American president, Franklin Roosevelt, had hoped that the French would relinquish Indochina as the British were planning to relinguish India; but there was a vital difference. The British had themselves resolved to leave India as soon as the transfer of power could decently be arranged. The French were determined to return to Indochina.

In April 1945 Roosevelt died and his successor, Harry S. Truman, was at the same time less committed to the anti-colonial cause than Roosevelt and more concerned about the developing rivalry between America and the Soviet Union in Europe and elsewhere (ibid., pp. 5–7). It is arguable that Ho Chi Minh was a nationalist first and a communist second, but his years in Moscow (he had returned there in the 1930s) made him very suspect in American eyes. It was a grave blow to American policy and a great shock to American opinion, which had always regarded China as a protégé, when the communist forces of Mao Tse-Tung finally defeated the nationalist forces of Chiang Kai-shek there in 1949. The 'domino theory', that one state after another would fall to the communists, was already being applied to South-East Asia.

In the circumstances, the Americans hoped that the French would hold the line in Indochina. It had been arranged in the summer of 1945 that British forces should occupy the southern half of Vietnam, the nationalist Chinese the north, until the French should return. In fact, in Vietnam, as in Indochina, Mountbatten had temporarily to rely upon the Japanese to continue to maintain order. When the French troops under General Leclerc arrived in the spring of 1946, Mountbatten told him bluntly that he saw little future for the French in Indochina, but Leclerc replied that he had his orders.

In effect Leclerc's first task was to reconquer north Vietnam, a supposedly peaceful agreement with Ho Chi Minh in March 1946 having broken down. On 23 November 1946 a French cruiser shelled the northern port of Haiphong. Six thousand people died. Ho Chi Minh and his forces 'went underground' (Grimal, 1978, p. 243). The French tried the experiment of restoring the emperor, Bao-Dai. Bao-Dai is usually condemned as a mere playboy, more familiar with the casinos of the French Riviera than with his own country; yet Herring is probably right in suggesting that he was neither unintelligent nor unpatriotic, but that his position as a French puppet made it impossible for him to rally any Vietnamese nationalists of consequence to his side (Herring, 1979, p. 15).

The French hoped to defeat the guerrillas as Templer had defeated the insurgents in Malaya, but once again the vital difference between an alien movement and one supported by at least a large section of the people became apparent. The communist victory in China in 1949 made it much easier for the guerrillas to get supplies and they began to extend their activities to Laos and Cambodia. The French determined to bring them to open battle. The result was, from the French point of view, disastrous. In the spring of 1954, 16,000 French troops (many of them from the prestigious Foreign Legion) were cut off at Dien Bien Phu and eventually, on 7 May, compelled to surrender to the Vietminh forces under General Giap.

Even before the defeat at Dien Bien Phu, the French had decided that they must cut their losses in Indochina. Technically, Laos had become an independent state in 1949 and Cambodia (Kampuchia), which had been an 'Associated State' since 1949, became fully independent in November 1953 – although this independence did not save either state from continuing to be drawn into the maelstrom of conflict in the region.

The Americans in particular now saw the struggle in Vietnam not primarily as one of decolonization but as one of resistance to communism. On the other hand, the French plainly could not continue to hold the line. Some alternative settlement must be found. There was already sitting at Geneva a conference of the foreign ministers of Russia, China, Britain and the United States, trying to find some way to end the Korean war which had been going on since 1950. The Indochina problem was referred to them. A cease-fire was arranged along the 17th parallel of latitude. The territory north of that line was by now under the control of the Vietminh. South of the line the French were to remain temporarily in possession, but with a promise to the Vietnamese of imminent independence. It was agreed that elections should take place throughout Vietnam within two years. The elections were never held. Instead, two states emerged divided by the 17th parallel. In the South, the French transferred power from Bao-Dai to a new head of state, Ngo Ding Diem. It was to prove another bad choice. Although some western observers may have been deceived (Smith, 1968, pp. 3–5) into identifying non-communist nationalism in Vietnam too closely with Buddhism (mainly through the spectacular suicide by burning of several Buddhist monks), the Catholic and Francophile Diem was, like Bao-Dai himself, quite unable to rally genuine popular support.

Diem was overthrown in 1963. Before that, the Americans had been drawn increasingly into supplying arms and advisers to keep his regime in existence. After 1964 the war escalated. In February 1965, the United States began the bombing of North Vietnam; in July of that year President Lyndon Johnson authorized the commitment of substantial American ground forces to the campaign. American involvement lasted until 1973 when President Nixon ordered the withdrawal of all American forces. By then American public opinion had totally turned against the war. In those eight years, more than 55,000 American soldiers were killed; the Vietnamese dead, both north and south, totalled well in excess of half a million.

Without American help, the Republic of South Vietnam held out for only two years. Surrender came in May 1975. Saigon was renamed Ho Chi Minh City, and North and South Vietnam were formally reunited as the Socialist Republic of Vietnam in 1976.

6

The Empires of the Smaller European Powers

The Dutch Empire

One traditional colonizing power, the Dutch, remained aloof from the scramble for colonies in the late nineteenth century. Apart from some remnants of empire in the Caribbean, the Dutch were content with their empire in Indonesia, the Dutch East Indies. It was a very rich area. In the sixteenth century, the Spice Islands, as they were then known – Java, Sumatra, Celebes, the Moluccas and part of Borneo – were the object of intense European competition. In the mid-nineteenth century, under the 'Culture System', by which the islanders were compelled to pay their taxes in the form of lucrative cash crops, the Dutch East Indies underpinned the whole Dutch economy. The system was ended in 1870, partly as the result of humanitarian protests that it was giving rise to conditions not far short of slavery.

Dutch administrative practice approximated more to the English system of indirect rule than to the French concept of the civilizing mission although, by the early twentieth century, under the influence of the so-called 'ethical policy', the Dutch had accepted some responsibility for introducing an education system. This system was not entirely welcomed by the Indonesian nationalists who had already begun to set up their own schools. The existence of a national movement had first become apparent in Java in 1908 (at about the same time as a similar movement was establishing itself in Indochina), although its immediate objectives seemed to be economic and cultural rather than political. In the 1920s it became more overtly political, and the Dutch suppressed it with some vigour. One of the political leaders to emerge at this time was Achmed Sukarno, later to be president of Indonesia.

But it was the Japanese occupation from 1942 to 1945 which, as in other parts of Asia, supplied the immediate stimulus for later nationalism. This worked in two rather contradictory ways. On the one hand, the British and the Americans encouraged guerrilla movements against the Japanese; these could, after the war, equally well be turned against the Dutch. On the other, the Japanese themselves encouraged a form of Indonesian nationalism, anti-European in character and based on the strong Islamic tradition in the archipelago, in which Sukarno played something of the same role as Aung San in Burma.

In August 1945 the Indonesian Republic was proclaimed in Batavia (Jakarta). As in Indochina, the Americans and the British – the latter had occupied the islands on the Japanese surrender – would have preferred to see an immediate arrangement with the nationalists in *de facto* control; but the Dutch, like the French, were determined to come back, although they were prepared to offer the Indonesians internal autonomy within what would have been some kind of Dutch commonwealth.

The offer was not sufficient to tempt Sukarno and a confused state of hostilities ensued, not only between the Dutch and the Indonesians but also between rival Indonesian groups. In November 1946, by the Linggadjati agreement, the Dutch recognized the Republic of Java and Sumatra and both sides agreed to work for a wider Indonesian federation which would form a union with the Netherlands under the Dutch Crown, that is, the 'commonwealth' solution again. The agreement broke down but it was now considered an international matter by some of Indonesia's neighbours, and in July 1947 India and Australia brought the matter before the Security Council of the United Nations.

Further fighting followed, and only in August 1949 did the Netherlands recognize the full independence of the Indonesian Republic. In 1963 Western New Guinea (Irian Jaya) was added to its territories but the government faced strong separatist movements there and in Sumatra and Celebes; and the 1960s also saw fighting between Indonesia and newly independent Malaya for certain disputed regions. In 1975 the Indonesians seized the island of Timor from the decaying Portuguese empire. Sukarno remained president until he was overthrown by an army coup in 1967 which brought General Suharto to power. Sukarno died in 1970. Suharto retained power until 1998. The United Nations never recognized the validity of the Indonesian annexation of East Timor and fierce fighting has continued there. Religious issues complicate the situation. Indonesia is predominantly Muslim but in both East Timor and Ambon (in the Moluccas) the majority population is Christian. Indonesian actions have been condemned by world opinion and, since the fall of Suharto, the Indonesian government has indicated some willingness to negotiate on the East Timor question.

The Belgian Empire

The Belgians, or more strictly their king, Leopold II, had been inspired to seek an empire by the financial success of the Dutch in Indonesia. After various unsuccessful attempts elsewhere Leopold had managed to establish a colony in the Congo basin, recognized as the Congo Free State by the great powers after the Berlin West African Conference in 1885. It became the scene of the worst colonial exploitation of the period, variously exposed by E. D. Morel in *Red Rubber* (1906), by Joseph Conrad in *Heart of Darkness* (1902) and by Roger Casement in his reports to the British government. The scandal became so great that, in 1908, the Belgian parliament was forced to assume responsibility for the Congo as an ordinary colony – it had previously been a kind of royal fief.

In 1955 an eminent Belgian journalist could describe the Congo as 'the most prosperous and tranquil of colonies' (Gifford and Louis, 1982, p. 305). Its prosperity was real, due to its great mineral resources, but its tranquillity was illusory. Basically what the writer meant was that, unlike other parts of Africa, the Congo had as yet produced no significant nationalist movement. This was partly attributable to the different approach to education in the Congo. Largely in the hands of missionary societies, it had been almost entirely practical and vocational. At the technical level it had in fact been good. On independence the Congo had more skilled artisans than many former colonies but it had only sixteen university graduates, no doctors, no lawyers and no engineers (ibid., p. 307).

In India, the evolution of a modern state took at least a century: in Ghana a generation. In the Congo, the whole process was packed into four years. It is hardly surprising that it was fraught with disaster. In fact the Congolese had started to take an interest in the rapid political developments in the neighbouring French colonies in the mid-1950s. The liberal–socialist coalition government which came into office in Belgium in 1954 began to make tentative political advances in the Congo. Municipal elections were held there for the first time in 1957 and one Congolese party, ABAKO (*Alliance des Bakongo*), led by Joseph Kasvubu, was sufficiently well organized to make an impressive showing.

In 1958 the liberal–socialist coalition in Brussels fell. At much the same time the world price of copper, the Congo's principal export, suddenly dropped. The region was plunged into economic crisis. Belgian politics were far from stable and it was increasingly clear that Belgium was not prepared to undertake the risk and expense of trying to govern a reluctant Congo. In the summer of 1958 General de Gaulle made a speech, not unlike Macmillan's 'wind of change' speech, in the Senegalese capital of Dakar, which seems to have attracted particular attention in the Congo. Later in 1958 a Congolese, Patrice Lumumba, the leader of the *Mouvement National Congolais*, visited Accra as a delegate to the All-African Conference. He returned to the Congo in January 1959 to announce that their objective was immediate independence. Serious riots followed in the Congolese capital, Leopoldville, which were partly economic, partly political in origin. The colonial authorities suppressed them but, ironically, almost simultaneously the king, Baudouin II, was announcing on Belgian radio that the Congo was to be given its independence. The timetable was worked out at a conference in Brussels early in 1960, while the riots in the Congo grew worse. Power was finally transferred on 30 June 1960 to the Democratic Republic of the Congo (known as Zaire from 1971 to 1997).

Its early days were extremely stormy. Most of the political parties, which had been hastily formed in the last days of colonial rule, were based on tribal and regional loyalties. The Congo, like most European colonies in Africa, had been an artificial construction. Soon after independence the army mutinied and Moise Tshombe, who had favoured a federal constitution, declared Katanga to be an independent republic. A state of civil war ensued in which atrocities were committed, some of them against Europeans. On 11 July Belgian paratroopers intervened and Lumumba asked for a United Nations force. This force returned Katanga to Congo control, but Lumumba himself was killed in December 1960. Tshombe gained control of the whole country from 1963 to 1965 but was overthrown by an army coup, led by General Mobutu, in November 1965.

The violence and civil war in the Congo made a lasting impression on European opinion; but still more on the white minorities of South Africa and Southern Rhodesia, who became convinced that black majority rule was a prescription for anarchy. Events in the Congo were thus a major factor in Rhodesia's unilateral declaration of independence.

After the First World War Belgium received part of the former German East Africa adjacent to the Belgian Congo as the mandated territory of Ruanda-Urundi, which it continued to administer as a United Nations trusteeship territory after the Second World War. In 1959 the majority Hutu population turned against the ruling Tutsis. Massacres followed and many Tutsis fled to Uganda. After United Nations' intervention, the Belgian trusteeship was ended in 1962 and two independent states, Rwanda and Burundi, were created. But fighting continued and reached genocidal proportions. In 1994 Hutu militia killed half a million Tutsis and moderate Hutus. Millions of refugees fled into neighbouring countries, threatening to destabilize the whole region.

The Italian Empire

Unlike the other belligerents Italy lost her empire as a direct result of the Second World War. They, after all, had ultimately been on the winning side. Italy was a defeated enemy.

The Italian empire was of recent construction. Not long before the First World War, Italy had acquired Libya from the decaying

Ottoman empire. Her attempt to conquer Abyssinia had ended disastrously at the battle of Adowa in 1896, the only major defeat suffered by a European power at African hands in the course of the Scramble. She had, however, made good her claim to Eritrea and Italian Somaliland. The Italians were bitterly disappointed by their failure to make more colonial gains as a result of the First World War, and Mussolini's conquest of Abyssinia (successful this time) in the 1930s was an effort to remedy this, as well as a fanciful attempt to build a new Roman empire.

Abyssinia (Ethiopia) had been a member of the League of Nations before the Italian invasion and, when the Italians were driven out in 1941, the country was immediately restored to independence under its emperor, Haile Selassie. He continued to rule until overthrow by a revolution in 1972. Eritrea remained under British protection until 1952, when it was given to Ethiopia. After a long struggle Eritrea separated from Ethiopia in 1993 but border disputes remain. Italian Somaliland (Somalia) was united with British Somaliland in 1960 to form the Somali Democratic Republic. The armed forces seized control in 1969 but, in 1991, the country was torn apart by rival war lords. An attempted United Nations' intervention proved disastrous.

In Libya the Italians had encouraged Italian immigration and briefly, before the Second World War, tried to govern some of the country as the French did Algeria, as part of the Italian mainland. After the war it was placed partly under British, partly under French, administration, rather as the successor states of the Ottoman empire had been in 1919. It became independent on 24 December 1951, with a monarchical form of government under King Idris. Idris was overthrown in September 1969 by Colonel Qadhafi.

The Spanish Empire

Spain had lost most of her empire at the time of the Napoleonic wars and some of the rest, the Philippines and Cuba, in the Spanish–American war in 1898; but in 1945 she still had a small remnant of an empire in Africa.

Spanish Morocco was united with the rest of Morocco in 1956.

The territory further south, Spanish Sahara (Rio de Oro), proved a greater problem. In February 1976 Spain relinquished all rights to it; but the northern part became disputed territory between Morocco and the Republic of Mauritania, one of the successor states of French West Africa.

Rio Muni, Fernando Po and a few small islands joined together in 1968 to form the new state of Equatorial Guinea. For some time it received some economic assistance from Nigeria but this was withdrawn in the late 1970s, leaving a scarcely viable state.

The Portuguese Empire

The Portuguese empire was the first of the European maritime empires, dating from the end of the fifteenth century. It was also destined to be the last. Portugal's great colony of Brazil became independent in 1822. By the nineteenth century, her African empire was moribund; but it revived during the Scramble, and in 1945 she still had two important colonies on the African continent, Angola and Mozambique. She had no intention of relinquishing either of these. The situation was complicated by the fact that the Portuguese had been far less racially exclusive than the northern Europeans, and had intermarried comparatively freely; many of the inhabitants of its colonies were therefore of mixed race.

The Portuguese theory of empire approximated, at least in some respects, to that of France. There was a sense of civilizing mission, expressed usually in the spreading of Catholic Christianity. Not much attention was paid to education, but the Portuguese recognized a category of *assimilado* (similar to the French *évolué*), that is to say educated Africans, ready for the grant of full citizenship. The numbers involved were small. In 1950 there were 30,000 such citizens in Angola (in a population of some four million) and only just over 4,000 in Mozambique in a population of over five million (Hatch, 1965, p. 236). But, most importantly, the Portuguese saw future development as lying in the closer union of the colonies with the metropolitan power and certainly not in devolution or independence. This philosophy suited admirably the authoritarian government of Dr Salazar, who had ruled Portugal since 1932.

In June 1951 the Salazar government decreed that the colonies were henceforth 'Overseas Provinces'. During the next two decades the white settler population, far from declining, grew rapidly, particularly in Angola (Gifford and Louis, 1982, p. 339). Urbanization increased and so did tensions between black Africans and white settlers, especially as many of the newcomers were 'poor whites', in direct economic competition with the Africans. In 1959 mounting economic pressures led to a strike in the small Portuguese West African territory of Guinea-Bissau. A number of Africans were killed in clashes with the police.

It was impossible for the Portuguese territories to remain immune from the unrest and the growing sense of nationalism which was sweeping over Africa by the 1960s. The Portuguese made some reforms in 1961–2, notably abolishing the requirement for forced labour which could still be imposed upon Africans; but this was quite inadequate for the temper of the times.

The first serious uprising was in northern Angola in February 1961 when the prison of Sao Paulo de Luanda was attacked. The authorities were the more frightened because of what was happening to the north in the Congo. Indeed they believed that further attacks on white settlers the following month had been carried out by irregulars from over the Congolese border. They retaliated with all the military force at their command. Casualties have been estimated at between 20,000 and 60,000 dead (Figueiredo, 1975, pp. 209–10). The rebellion spread to Mozambique.

In the Portuguese empire, even more than in the French, the end came in full-scale war. Salazar had gambled everything on making metropolitan Portugal, itself a poor country, the centre of a rich empire. Investment, as well as immigration, had been encouraged. For a time Portugal not only obtained sugar, coffee and tea for herself from her African colonies but balanced her budget by exporting them. Beira in Mozambique was one of the most prosperous ports in southern Africa, serving Northern and Southern Rhodesia and the Transvaal, as well as Mozambique itself.

In the end the colonies destroyed, not saved, the regime which Salazar had so carefully built up. Salazar himself died in 1970 (he had been incapacitated since 1968); but his successors continued his policy for a few more years until both the economic cost and the drain on Portugal's own human resources became intolerable. Men were constantly recalled to the colours to go and fight in the colonies. Finally, the government was overthrown by a military coup in April 1974. For two years Portugal lived on the brink of further revolution. The colonies were the immediate beneficiaries. Guinea-Bissau became independent on 10 September 1974, Mozambique on 25 June 1975 and Angola on 11 November 1975.

As with the other European empires, it soon became apparent that many problems had begun, rather than ended, with independence. Guinea-Bissau soon succumbed to a military coup. In Mozambique a one-party state was established by the Marxist Liberation Movement, Frelimo (*Frente de Libertacao de Mocambique*) but this was challenged by Mozambican National Resistance (Renamo). The civil war continued until 1992. After United Nations' intervention multi-party elections were held in 1994. But it was Angola which suffered most. Civil war, as well as war against the Portuguese, was raging when independence came. Cuban assistance enabled the Marxist MPLA (*Movimento Popular de Libertação de Angola*) to gain control in 1976 and to form a one-party state; but the rebel movement, Unita, with some South African backing, again created a situation of civil war. A cease-fire was arranged in 1998 but war was resumed in 1993. The United Nations mediated the Lusaka Protocol between the MPLA and Unita in 1994 but peace has not yet (1999) been completely restored.

7

The Russian Empire

In 1989 the Russian dissident Andrei Sakharov called the Soviet Union 'the last empire on the planet' (Royal Institute of International Affairs, 20 June 1989). Like some of the European maritime empires it had taken centuries to construct but, like the American empire, it was a land empire. An early twentieth-century encyclopedia had no doubts about the similarities. Describing the foundation of Russia, it said, 'From their capital of Kiev, the grand princes of the house of Rurik gradually absorbed under one system the great plain. The process was the same as that which carried the American people farther and farther west' (Harmsworth, Vol. 8, 1923, p. 6,770) The original state was broken up by the Mongol invasions of the thirteenth century. In 1492 the Tsar, Ivan III, established his capital at Moscow. Kiev was controlled in turn by various groups, including the Lithuanians, the Hungarians and the Poles but, in 1667, Poland ceded it to Russia.

A generation later Russia was expanding into the Baltic region. Peter the Great built his new capital, St Petersburg, on the Gulf of Finland. He also acquired Estonia and most of Latvia in his wars with Sweden. Lithuania became Russian during the Partitions of Poland at the end of the eighteenth century. But the three Baltic states always felt a sense of separateness from Russia, which expressed itself partly in religious terms. The Lithuanians, like the Poles, were Roman Catholics. The Latvians and Estonians, who had been part of the Hanseatic League and had strong associations with Germany, were mainly Protestant. They did not identify with the Orthodox Church, with its Patriarch in Moscow, which was a major unifying force in Russia.

South of Lithuania lay what is now Belarus, sometimes called White Russia. It had been part of the Kievian state in the ninth century but it had been absorbed into Lithuania in the thirteenth and fourteenth centuries, passing under Polish rule in the sixteenth. It was transferred to Russia by the Partitions of Poland and remained Russian even when the Kingdom of Poland was restored in 1815.

In the eighteenth century Russia expanded southwards. Catherine the Great took the Crimea region from the Tatars (Mongols) in the 1770s and the Ukraine, which had long had close relations with Russia, was absorbed into the empire. Other wars with Turkey and Persia brought eastern Armenia and northern Azerbaijan in. Both had been part of the classical world. Armenia was the oldest Christian state in the world, declaring Christianity its official religion in 301, eleven years before the conversion of the Roman emperor, Constantine. By the sixteenth century it had been incorporated into the Ottoman empire but the Armenians retained their Christian faith and in the 1890s and during the First World War, one and a half million of those who remained under Turkish rule were massacred – in proportion to population as great a holocaust as that of the Jews during the Second World War. In Azerbaijan the original population had been largely displaced and Islam had become the dominant religion by about 1000 AD, apart from the enclave of Nagorny-Karabakh, where a distinct Armenian population survived. Georgia, predominantly Orthodox Christian and lying just north of Armenia and Azerbaijan, with an important Black Sea coast, turned to Russia for protection against the Ottomans and was eventually incorporated into the Russian empire in the early nineteenth century.

During the eighteenth century too Russia had begun her long eastward march to the Pacific, the movement which most closely resembled America's westward expansion. Many in the nineteenth century saw Siberia as a colony, not dissimilar to the British colonies of settlement. The German colonial propagandist, Friedrich Fabri, commended it to his fellow countrymen as a successful experiment as a penal colony (Breuning, 1998, pp. 100–5). By 1732 Russia had acquired the Kamchatka Peninsula. She did not stop at the ocean. In 1741 she took Alaska (which she sold to be United States in 1867). In the late nineteenth century she established herself in the Amur region (Vladivostock was founded in 1860) and, in the early twentieth century, she occupied northern Manchuria. Mongolia also came within the Russian sphere, although not technically part of the empire.

The middle of the nineteenth century saw a surge of Russian activity in Central Asia. Russian expansion there had begun in the eighteenth century for a variety of reasons, trade, appeals from various groups, for example the Kazakhs, for help against their enemies, perhaps mainly – as British writers speculated in the nineteenth century – from the natural tendency of an empire to expand until it comes up against an insuperable barrier, either a geographical one or an equally powerful empire. It was Russian moves in Central Asia which began to alert the British to an possible threat to their own Indian empire. Kazakhstan was acquired early (in 1731) but Uzbekistan and what are now Turkmenistan and Kyrgystan came later at various dates in the nineteenth century.

It was obvious from the beginning that Central Asia would be more difficult to absorb than most of the eastern lands, which were sparsely populated, or the gains in the south-west, where the populations often had ethnic, religious and linguistic ties with Russia. Central Asia was inhabited by peoples quite distinct from the Russians and predominantly Muslim in faith. In tsarist times the government of the region was essentially colonial, often military, and readily recognized as such by the colonial powers of Western Europe.

The triumph of the communist (Bolshevik) revolution in 1917 created a much more complicated situation. The revolution and the civil war which followed gave those regions which wished to break away the chance to do so. The most successful break for freedom was that of the Baltic states. Estonia, Latvia and Lithuania gained the recognition of the new League of Nations for their recovered status as independent nations. Republics such as Georgia and Armenia lasted only as long as the chaos of the civil war, which in some cases also saw the intervention of third parties. Britain, France, Japan and the United States intervened to halt the Bolsheviks; Turkey and Poland in pursuit of old quarrels.

An Azerbaijan Democratic Republic was established in 1918 but was quickly overthrown by Soviet forces and Azerbaijan was incorporated into the Soviet Union in 1922. Armenia was fiercely fought over by the Soviets and the Turks. It first declared its independence in May 1918, and again in 1921, but on each occasion the Armenians were defeated and in 1922 the part which Russia controlled acceded to the Soviet Union. In Georgia a nationalist government came to power after the Bolshevik revolution and received support from the West but in 1921 Soviet forces occupied the capital, Tbilisi, and Georgia was incorporated into the Transcaucasian Soviet Socialist Republic in 1922.

A number of the Central Asian territories also saw fighting during the civil war. Kazakhstan was under White (tsarist) Russian control for a time but became a Soviet Socialist Republic (SSR) in August 1920. Uzbekistan was divided in its allegiances. In November 1917 a communist revolution broke out in Tashkent and parts of Uzbekistan were incorporated into the Turkestan SSR in 1918, but most of Uzbekistan wished to be independent in the old units of Khiva and Bokhara. They were defeated by the Red (communist) army and Soviet rule was established in 1921. Soviet control was established early in Turkmenistan, in April 1918, but civil war then broke out. Turkmenistan was strategically important and had oil resources and British forces intervened from India and Persia (Iran). The Red army, however, prevailed and Turkmenistan became an SSR in February 1925. Kyrgystan passed under Soviet control in 1920.

In the East there was fighting in both Mongolia and Manchuria but in 1924 the Soviet Union had to acknowledge Chinese suzerainty in Mongolia, and Manchuria too passed out of the Soviet sphere of influence (which, in the North, had survived Russia's defeat by Japan in 1905).

By 1922 the new Soviet Union had recovered most of the old tsarist empire. The nucleus of the Soviet Union, which was formed on 30 December 1922, consisted of the four SSRs of Russia, the Ukraine, Byelorussia (Belarus) and Transcaucasia (Azerbaijan, Georgia and Armenia). In 1918 significant parts of the new state had been under German occupation and the Treaty of Brest Litovsk of March 1918 had ceded most of the Ukraine to Germany and compelled Russia to recognize the independence of the rest. The Ukraine was a major battlefield during the civil war but the Soviets gradually gained control. Much of Belarus was occupied by Germany at the time of the revolution in 1917. When Germany withdrew at the end of the war, the Byelorussian SSR was proclaimed in 1919 but Poland then went to war with Russia to recover her own lost territories. Against a greatly weakened Russia, the new Polish state was able to extend its boundaries beyond the limits of the ethnic Polish population and, in 1920, Russia had to cede western Belarus to Poland.

The Union of Soviet Socialist Republics (USSR) – Russia's official title until 1991 – was formed in 1923. In form it was a voluntary association of independent socialist republics. The 1923 constitution provided for the adhesion of other like-minded republics and, in theory, for member republics to secede. This right of secession was preserved in the subsequent 1936 and 1977 constitutions. Russia took advantage of this nominal independence of the various republics to ask for separate membership for each of them in the United Nations, claiming that they were as independent of Moscow as Canada and Australia were by this time of London. The argument did not carry conviction and the United Nations accepted the claims only of the Ukraine and Byelorussia.

In fact the Soviet republics enjoyed nothing like the freedom of the British dominions and certainly did not (and were never intended to have) the same potential for independence and distinctive growth. The concept of nationalism was an embarrassment to communist thought. It was a primitive feudal or bourgeois concept, which should have been overtaken by the solidarity of the workers. This provided a convenient mechanism for the retention of central control. Each of the republics was, in reality, governed by the Communist Party and each regional Communist Party was closely linked to Moscow.

Russians had a significant ethnic, as well as cultural and political, presence in many of the republics. Sometimes, as in the Baltic states, this was a deliberately pursued policy, reinforced by the movement of populations. (For the Baltic states, see below, pp. 109–10). Sometimes the Russian minority was a small one; 6 or 7 per cent in Georgia, Azerbaijan or Turkmenistan for example –

although it often carried with it the right to use Russian as an official language. Sometimes it was much larger; 21 per cent in Kyrgystan or even 36 per cent in Kazakhstan. It was comparatively modest in the Ukraine (22 per cent) or Belarus (13 per cent) but similarities of language, culture and shared history gave Russia a strong voice.

The Second World War enabled Russia again to take control of the Baltic states. The Molotov–Ribbentrop Pact between the Soviet Union and Nazi Germany in August 1939 allowed Russia to take Latvia, Estonia, Lithuania and part of Poland in return for acquiesence in German plans. The USSR took all these countries in 1940. A fig leaf of legality was provided by the supposed consent of the workers. Germany occupied the Baltic states after Germany and Russia went to war in 1941 but Russia regained them in 1944. The Russian acquisition of Estonia, Latvia and Lithuania was never recognized by most of the United Nations. The Molotov–Ribbentrop Pact also allowed the Soviet Union to seize the Romanian province of Bessarabia and it was duly 'liberated' on 28 June 1940 and renamed Moldavia.

The fall of the Soviet empire may perhaps be used to illustrate two ancient truisms; the first being that an over-extended empire is an empire in danger. That had been eloquently expressed by Sir William Harcourt in 1892, when counselling against any further extension of the British empire in Africa. Quoting with approval Edward Gibbon's praise of the 'moderation of Augustus' in not over-extending the Roman empire, he warned, 'If you give the heart too much work to do by extending the limbs and the frame beyond measure you enfeeble its action, and it succumbs' (quoted in Bennett, 1962, p. 309; Gardiner vol. 2, p. 196). The second truism is that the most dangerous moment for a bad regime is when it begins to reform itself.

Arguably the over-extension began at the end of the Second World War. Russia had suffered terribly during that war. Her casualties had included nearly 8 million civilian dead, as well as over 13 million military personnel killed or missing. After the war the Russians, however unjustifiably, feared another armed attack from the capitalist West. One safeguard seemed to be the acquisition of their own nuclear weapons and the upkeep of a great military machine – ultimately too expensive for the ailing Soviet economy. The other safeguard was the erection of a defensive bulwark of satellite states in eastern Europe and the Balkans.

Although the Red army was in physical control of much of eastern Europe at the end of the Second World War, its political acquisition was not straightforward and, in some cases, took several years to accomplish. The Allied powers had agreed at summit conferences during the war, at Yalta and elsewhere, that free elections must be held in the countries liberated from German rule. Although communist parties existed in eastern Europe and the Balkans, and had often played an honourable part in the defeat of Nazi Germany, they knew that they could not rely on democratic processes to bring them to power.

Poland was the key country. Much of Poland had been under Russian direct rule as a result of the eighteenth-century partitions. 'Congress' Poland, created by the Congress of Vienna at the end of the Napoleonic wars, had been a Russian satellite. Poland had taken its revenge at the end of the First World War, biting deep into Russian territory. Russia now reclaimed what she believed to be hers, plus a slice of Poland and part of East Prussia, ancient German territory. Poland got the rest of East Prussia, as well as the inter-war 'Polish corridor', intended to give Poland an outlet to the Baltic, which included the great Hansa port of Danzig, now Gdansk. Russia presided over massive population movements, designed to remove Germans from East Prussia. It was essentially ethnic cleansing, although carried out by population exchanges rather than by massacres and it passed almost unnoticed by the outside world in the chaos of Europe at the end of the Second World War, when there were already several million 'displaced persons' mainly in Germany.

In the closing stages of the war there had been two rival claimants to be recognized as the Polish government once the Germans were expelled; the Polish government in exile in London and the 'Lublin' Poles, entirely under Russian influence. In its determination to control Poland, the Soviet Union was brutal. In April 1940 they had massacred 15,000 Polish officers, the natural leaders of their country, at Katyn and related sites, an atrocity for which they attempted to blame the Nazis until the facts became incontrovertible in the 1980s. As early as 1943 the Soviet leader, Joseph Stalin, had broken off relations with the Polish provisional government in London when they demanded an explanation.

In 1944 the Poles in Warsaw rose against the retreating Germans. Soviet forces held back until the Germans finally suppressed the rising in early October. In July 1944 the Soviet Union had recognized the Lublin Committee of Polish Liberation in Moscow as the legitimate authority for a liberated Poland. This should have been superseded by the arrangements supposedly put in place at Yalta in February 1945. According to these a Three Power Commission in Moscow would supervise the setting up of a Provisional Government, which would include London, as well as Lublin, Poles and free elections would be held as soon as possible. In fact in April 1945 the Soviets concluded a treaty of alliance with the Lublin Poles and, in July, Britain and the United States recognized a Provisional Government of National Unity (in reality a communist government) in Poland. It was to be 35 years before the communist grip on Poland was seriously challenged.

It took the communists a little longer to establish control in Czechoslovakia, another of Hitler's early victims, which had been widely regarded as a model democracy before the Second World War. A Provisional National Assembly met in October 1945, which included both communist and non-communist members. In elections in May 1946 the communists won 38 per cent of the vote but, in 1948, the democratic politicians were driven out. The Foreign Minister, Jan Masaryk, was probably murdered, although his death was given out as suicide. In June the veteran Eduard Beneš was compelled to resign as president, to be succeeded by the communist, Klement Gottwald.

Hungary's position was weakened by the fact that its right-wing pre-war government had signed the anti-Comintern Pact in 1939 and entered the war on the German side in 1941. A provisional government of liberation, with a large communist element, was formed in December 1944. Between 1945 and 1949 Hungary was governed by a coalition government of the Smallholder, National Peasant, Social Democrat and Communist parties. It concentrated on land reform, dismantling the great estates, which had been characteristic of pre-war Hungary. But, in 1949, the communists destroyed the Smallholder and National Peasant parties and compelled the Social Democrats to join them in the People's Front. The 1949 elections were conducted on single lists and the People's Front won nearly 96 per cent of the vote. Henceforth, Hungary was to be a one-party state.

The position in East Germany was more complicated. The Allies had divided defeated Germany into four zones, the American, British, French and Russian. The capital, Berlin, which was an enclave in the Russian part, was likewise divided into four zones. The arrangement was meant to be a temporary one until the fate of Germany was decided by the Allies and a peace treaty signed. Divisions between the Allies delayed that prospect indefinitely. In 1948 the Russians withdrew from the Control Council, through which the Allies had originally co-operated in their administration of Germany. Henceforth the Russians went their own way in their zone. In October 1949 a communist-controlled 'German Democratic Republic' was set up in what became known as East Germany. The previous year the (unsuccessful) Russian attempt to cut Berlin off from the West had led to the Berlin Airlift, by which the western allies supplied the city from the air. This in turn led to the setting up of the North Atlantic Treaty Organization (NATO) by the United States, Canada and their European allies, which was then to be confronted by the Warsaw Pact of Russia and her satellites, Czechoslovakia, the German Democratic Republic (GDR), Hungary, Poland, Albania, Bulgaria and Romania.

Since before the First World War the Balkans had seemed a natural area of expansion for Russia. Since at least 1829 Russia had felt that she stood in the position of patron to Romania (then the Principalities of Moldavia and Wallachia), which needed her protection against the Ottoman empire. In 1947 King Michael of Romania was compelled to abdicate and, in 1952, a new constitution modelled on the Soviet one (of 1936) was adopted. Like Hungary, Romania became a one-party state.

Bulgaria, which after it was constituted in 1878 maintained a fragile independence from tsarist Russia, tried to remain neutral in the Second World War. But, in September 1944, the Soviet Union refused to recognize such neutrality and declared war on Bulgaria, compelling the Bulgarians to seek an armistice and declare war on

Germany. The same month a *coup d'état* brought a coalition, including the communists, to power. In August 1945 the main non-communist parties left the government. A (probably rigged) referendum in 1946 abolished the monarchy and set up a republic. A new constitution was proclaimed in 1947. Other parties lingered for a short time but were then suppressed or absorbed into the Communist Party.

Two other countries, although communist, retained rather strange relationships with the USSR. Albania, a remote and inward-looking region even in Ottoman times, adopted such hard-line communism that it could not free itself from Stalinist influence and in the 1960s began to break away from Moscow (it left the Warsaw Pact in 1961) to find a more congenial patron in Mao-Tse-tung's China.

Yugoslavia had been an entirely artificial creation at the end of the First World War, made up of Serbia, Macedonia and Montenegro, which had earlier freed themselves from the Ottoman empire; parts of the former Austro-Hungarian empire, which later became Slovenia and Croatia; and Bosnia-Herzegovina, which Austria had taken from the Ottoman empire before the war. Yugoslavia had offered strong resistance to the Germans in the Second World War, despite deep divisions within the country. At the end of the war the communist leader, Marshal Tito, accomplished the apparently impossible by holding its diverse regions together, while at the same time establishing some degree of independence from Moscow. Yugoslavia was never part of the Warsaw Pact. Only after Tito's death in 1980 did the whole construct begin to fall apart along ancient fissures. Slovenia and Croatia were western in tradition and predominantly Catholic in religion; Serbia, Montenegro and Macedonia belonged to the Eastern Orthodox tradition; Bosnia and Herzegovina had a mixed Catholic, Orthodox and Muslim population.

In Russia itself the death of Stalin in 1953 led to the first loosening of the dictatorial regime, which had seen mass starvation among the peasants as a result of the ill-managed 'collectivization' of agriculure and the great purges, which had robbed the Soviet Union of its intellectuals, as well as destroying the officer corps of the army just before the Second World War. There was some improvement in relations with the West but it was not consistently maintained. The Cuban missile crisis of 1962 was possibly the most dangerous crisis of the whole Cold War period but talks were begun about the control of nuclear weapons, culminating in the Strategic Arms Limitation Talks (SALT), which produced an interim agreement in 1972.

But the real changes did not come until the 1980s in the era of perestroika and glasnost. It is this that may perhaps confirm the second truism, that the most dangerous moment for a bad regime is when it first risks reform. Within seven years the whole Soviet system had crumbled. Ronald Reagan, who became president of the United States in 1981, and the hard-line American right might like to take the credit for the effects of their uncompromising hostility to the 'evil empire'. But, in reality, the dissolution probably owed more to internal forces.

At first Nikita Kruschev (1953–64) and Leonid Brezhnev (1964–82) provided reasonably strong, if sometimes eccentric, leadership after the death of Stalin. But from 1982 to 1985 Russia was incompetently led by the very elderly Yuri Andropov and then by the equally decrepit Konstantin Chernenko. It could only be seen as a period of marking time while the Russian economy decayed.

The economy was further strained and Russian pride and self-confidence deeply wounded by the disastrous intervention in Afghanistan, which dated from Brezhnev's declining years. In the nineteenth century Afghanistan had been a bone of contention between Russia and Britain, defending her Indian empire. Britain had suffered more than one disaster there. In the end both sides had been prepared to settle for a 'hands off' policy, which allowed an independent Afghanistan to act as a buffer state between British India and Russian Central Asia. After the Second World War Afghanistan was, at least in theory, a constitutional monarchy but this was overthrown by a *coup d'état* in 1973. In turn President Daoud, who had been elected president of the republic in 1977, was overthrown by the army the following year. Afghanistan was drifting into civil war and neighbouring Pakistan as well as the Soviet Union were fishing in troubled waters. In December 1979 Soviet forces invaded Afghanistan. Afghanistan is ideal guerrilla country and the Soviets finally agreed to withdraw in 1988, having suffered 15,000 fatal casualties (mainly young conscripts) and achieved none of their objectives.

In March 1985 the energetic and comparatively young (he was 53) Mikhail Gorbachev became First Secretary of the Communist Party of the Soviet Union, that is head of the executive – a role closer to that of the president of the United States than to that of a European prime minister. Gorbachev in fact became Executive President in 1990. From the first he determined to carry out the radical overhaul of the Soviet system and the Soviet economy, which had for so long been needed. He proclaimed 'perestroika', literally 'restructuring'. In practice it meant decentralization and the admission of market forces into what had previously been a 'command' economy. It was to be coupled with, indeed to some extent driven by, 'glasnost', that is, 'openness'. For the first time for nearly seventy years, free discussion of almost all issues was to be permitted. Whether Gorbachev meant the changes to go as far as they did or not, once the lid was off, there was no possibility of replacing it.

Understandably, the first effects were felt in what might be called Russia's 'European empire'. The Russians, who had always been used under the tsars to authoritarian government and a high incidence of poverty and subsistence economy, had tolerated communism with little more than the wry subversive joke. It was different in the satellites and in the Baltic states, which had at least tasted political and cultural freedom and often enjoyed a good degree of material prosperity between the wars.

There had been some insurrections earlier. In June 1953, not long after the death of Stalin, workers had risen in various parts of East Germany but had been put down by the security police. There was a similar but smaller rising by workers demanding better conditions in Poland in June 1956. But the most serious rising, this time overtly political, was in Hungary in October 1956. The new prime minister, Imre Nagy, announced Hungary's withdrawal from the Warsaw Pact and asked the United Nations to recognize Hungary's neutrality. This rising was put down by Soviet forces and Nagy himself executed. The rest of the world was distracted at this time by the Suez crisis (see pp. 61–2) but western intervention would in any case have been improbable. A precarious status quo had been arrived at, not unlike the nineteenth concept of the balance of power. Areas were recognised as being in either the communist or the western sphere of influence and overt intervention was rare. (Similar considerations made Russia abandon Cuba in 1962.) It was cynical but, in a world where the alternative might well be a nuclear holocaust, it was also commonsensical. In 1968 Alexander Dubček's government tried to liberalize the Czech regime in the so-called 'Prague Spring'. In August Soviet troops, accompanied by token contingents from other Warsaw Pact powers, occupied the Czech capital and deposed Dubček. (Dubček, unlike Nagy, survived to see the final liberation of his country.)

The first sustained challenge to Soviet authority came from Poland, although its success or failure hung in the balance for nearly a decade. In June 1979 the visit of the Polish Pope John Paul II (Karol Wojtyla) gave the Poles an unprecedented opportunity to gather in large numbers and express their sense of national solidarity. Religion (Catholicism, as opposed to Orthodoxy) had always been a badge of Polish nationalism in their struggles with Russia, although it was economic discontents which finally triggered resistance. In 1980 there were widespread strikes against rising prices. The movement centred on the great shipyards at Gdansk. A previously unknown worker, Lech Walesa, emerged as the leader and the Poles demanded the recognition of free trade unions, collectively known as 'Solidarity', which by September had ten million members. At first the government bowed to the workers' demands. Ministers resigned, Solidarity was recognized, censorship was relaxed and the Church given new rights. But this was not to last. In February 1981 General Jaruzelski became prime minister and, in December, martial law was imposed, Solidarity banned and its leaders arrested. Martial law continued in force until the summer of 1983.

The relationship between Jaruzelski and Solidarity was in fact a complex one. Arguably both sides wished to maximize Polish independence but disagreed profoundly about tactics. In September 1986 Solidarity announced that it would work within the existing system to secure necessary changes but, in November 1987, it boycotted a referendum on radical reform. The year 1988 saw a wave of strikes and unrest across Poland and, for the first time since 1980, Solidarity felt strong enough to demand direct talks with the government. In December the government agreed to 'round table' talks with Solidarity.

The talks opened in February 1989. Solidarity was again legalized and the government agreed to free (or fairly free) elections. The elections were held in June – the elections promised at Yalta in 1945 but never implemented. To their own astonishment, Solidarity won a landslide victory. The communists were in disarray, despite being accorded various advantages, including virtual control of television during the election. Interestingly the Christian Democrats, although officially backed by the Polish Primate, did not do particularly well. By prior agreement with Solidarity, Jaruzelski was elected president.

In Hungary the first sign of change was the formal rehabilitation of the executed 1956 leader, Imre Nagy. In May 1989 the man who, backed by Soviet tanks, had replaced him, Janos Kadar, was forced to resign. A new constitution was proclaimed in October 1989 and free multi-party elections were held in March 1990.

In Czechoslovakia mass protests in November 1989 led to the resignation of the Communist Party Central Committee and, in December, a new government was formed in which only half the ministers were communists. Gustav Husák, who had been in power since 1969, resigned as president and was succeeded by the dissident playwright Václav Havel. The communists were defeated in the elections held in June 1990. On 1 January 1993 the Czech Republic and Slovakia split by mutual consent into two sovereign states.

In Bulgaria the communist leader Todor Zhivkov, who had been in power since 1971, was forced to resign in November 1989. Elections in June 1990 were won by the communist party, now calling itself the Bulgarian Socialist Party, but a few weeks later a multiparty government was formed.

Matters were more violent in Romania. In December 1989 mass demonstrations began in Timisoara and spread to Bucharest and other cities but here change was resisted by Nicolae Ceauşescu, who had been head of state since 1967. The Securitate (Secret Police) supported Ceauşescu but, after initial hesitation, the army joined the rebels. After some fighting and significant casualties, Ceauşescu was arrested and executed. Elections were held in May 1990 and a new constitution proclaimed in 1991.

East Germany was, arguably, Russia's most important satellite and here matters were complicated and, until a late stage, balanced on a knife edge. On the one hand the GDR had inevitably had contacts with West Germany, formalized by the so-called 'Basic Treaty' of 21 December 1972, and had the picture of the highly successful capitalist West Germany constantly before its eyes. Compared with other Eastern Bloc countries, its own economy was quite strong. On the other hand, its government under both Walter Ulbricht (1960–73) and Erich Honecker (1976–89) was a hard-line, almost Stalinist, one. Honecker's government resisted with horror the 'liberalization' and open discussion which was being encouraged in Gorbachev's Russia.

As in Poland, religion played some part. East Germany, unlike Poland, was predominantly Protestant – much of it consisted of the old Prussian lands. Church and state had found it expedient to reach compromises from 1958 onwards. As a result the churches were the only organizations which maintained some independence, in a society where the trade unions, cultural and even sporting associations were all communist dominated. In August 1989 four pastors from Greifswald and Halle began to plan an opposition social-democratic party. That same month the 'Monday' demonstrations began in the Nikolai Church in Leipzig, growing rapidly from a few hundred participants to many thousands and beginning to find echoes in other cities.

Overtly political groups, of which New Forum, associated with the name of Barbel Bohley, was one, sprang up. Honecker's government at first tried to suppress and ridicule such groups, boasting of the GDR's great achievements. Ironically, the Leipzig protesters appealed for the support of Mikhail Gorbachev in their support of perestroika. Gorbachev himself visited Berlin in October 1989 in connection with the 40th anniversary of the foundation of the GDR. His lukewarm support for Honecker and his vigorous endorsement of perestroika was clear to his auditors.

But the decisive factor was the 'Exodus'. In August 1961 the communists had erected the notorious Berlin Wall to prevent East Germans from escaping into West Berlin. Travel from all Soviet-controlled territories to the West was tightly regulated and made extremely difficult. In 1989 the 'Iron Curtain' suddenly became porous. In September Hungary opened its borders with Austria. It was mainly East Germans who poured through. At one point the calculation was made that one tenth of the population might leave. Even more alarmingly, it was the skilled and the professionals who were going.

Meanwhile demonstrations grew in East Germany itself. On 9 October over 50,000 demonstrated in Leipzig, shouting 'Wir sind das Volk' ('We are the people'). The demonstrations spread to Plauen, Potsdam and East Berlin, demanding the resignation of the government and free elections. The world waited, fearing another 'Tiananmen Square', where on 4 June 1989 the Chinese government had massacred those demonstrating for democracy in the Chinese capital. The forceful response never came. Even today it is not entirely clear why not. If it had, there would at the least have been civil war as in Romania. Mikhail Gorbachev's response may have been the decisive factor. He had made it clear that Soviet troops (there were still thousands stationed in East Germany) would not assist in repressing civil unrest. The communist government could still have relied on the Stasi (the secret police) and the *Kampfgruppen* (the security arm of the Party). A specific order to use force in Leipzig was countermanded at the last moment. Instead Honecker resigned on 18 October and was succeeded by Egon Krenz, another Politburo member. This attempt to keep control did not last long. On 7 November the government resigned. On 9 November free travel to the West was permitted and check-points in the Berlin Wall opened. Over the next few days the Wall was physically dismantled by the Berliners themselves.

David Keithly (1992, p. 1) quotes Aristotle at the beginning of his book on the collapse of East German communism: 'Hate is a passion all tyrants are bound to arouse: but contempt is often the cause by which tyrannies are actually overthrown'. In 1953 the German workers had backed down in the face of superior force. In 1989 the East German people stood their ground against a regime they now thoroughly despised. How much reason they had to despise it became apparent in the revelations of its corruption once the files were open. The slogan 'Wir sind das Volk' soon became 'Wir sind ein Volk' ('We are one people'). Economic union between East and West Germany began in July 1990. In September the GDR, the FDR and the four wartime allies, the United States, the Soviet Union, Britain and France, signed the 'Treaty on the Final Settlement with respect to Germany', reuniting East and West as a sovereign state from 3 October 1990. In the forty years of its existence the GDR had failed to establish itself as a nation state.

Gorbachev's hostility to the Stalinist Honecker and his refusal to intervene in East German affairs had opened the way for the re-unification and democratization of the whole of Germany. It could hardly be expected that he would take so sympathetic an attitude to the break-up of the Soviet Union itself.

In 1988 the Soviet Union began to crumble. The Baltic states were eager and ready to escape. If the pope's visit had heartened the Poles and perhaps made them feel still in touch with the West, it was modern communications which helped to trigger the move-ment in Estonia. Estonians had always been able to receive and understand Finnish television and it was a popular Estonian televi-sion programme in April 1988, modelled on western formats, which encouraged discussion and led to the setting up of what came to be called a 'Popular Front' to further perestroika – discussions to fur-ther perestroika were ideologically acceptable in Gorbachev's Rus-sia. Latvia and Lithuania followed Estonia's example. Latvia too had its 'Popular Front', Lithuania its 'Movement for Perestroika'.

Confidence grew quickly. In November 1988 the Estonian par-liament rejected amendments to the Soviet constitution, which would have increased Moscow's control. In February 1989 they raised their own national flag and flew it in preference to the ham-mer and sickle. But all the Baltic states had a particular problem in reasserting their national identity. The Soviet government had pur-sued a deliberate policy there as in Poland and East Prussia of popu-lation exchange. Many Balts had been compelled to move during the Second World War and a Russian population introduced dur-ing and after the war. Lithuania had been least affected, although about 20 per cent of its population was Russian or Polish. In Esto-nia where before the war 86 per cent of the population had been Estonian, with only about 8 per cent Russian, by the 1980s 40 per cent were non-Estonian, mainly Russian. In Latvia, where before the war there had been about 12 per cent Russians, by the 1980s barely 50 per cent of the population were Latvians. The very large Russian minorities were determined to preserve their position, in particular the official status of the Russian language. But at the end of the day Russian attempts to whip the Baltic states back into line were half-hearted compared to, say, their brutal intervention in Hungary in 1956.

Control over these supposedly 'independent' republics had always been through their communist parties. In December 1989 the Lithuanian Communist Party suddenly asserted genuine independence. It declared that it was a separate entity from the Communist Party of the Soviet Union and that its aim was 'an independent democratic Lithuanian state'. Gorbachev himself uttered threats and visited the Lithuanian capital, Vilnius. The television coverage further alerted everyone to what was happening. One banner particularly annoyed Gorbachev. It read 'We welcome the head of a neighbouring state' (Crawshaw, 1992, p. 111). In elections the following February the now openly pro-independence 'Movement' won. On 11 March 1990 the Lithuanian parliament voted overwhelmingly to resume their existence as a sovereign state 'annulled by an alien state in 1940' (ibid., p. 115).

The Soviet Union tried both economic sanctions and shows of military force to intimidate the Baltic states. In Latvia clashes with Russian troops led to some deaths in January 1991. The West, unwilling to destabilize Gorbachev, urged caution on the Balts. Nevertheless a national referendum in Latvia in March showed a nearly three to one majority in favour of independence. Multi-party elections in Estonia the same month showed the same result. In July Boris Yeltsin, the man destined to be in effect Gorbachev's successor and then president of Russia (as distinct from the Soviet Union) signed a treaty with the Lithuanians acknowledging for all practical purposes their separation from Russia. It was the failed coup against Gorbachev in August 1991 which led all three Baltic states to formally proclaim their independence. The Soviet Union finally recognized that independence on 10 September 1991.

The position of the Baltic states was exceptional. The majority of the world had never acknowledged the validity of the Russian annexation in 1940. But disaffection soon spread to areas which had been regarded as an integral part of the Soviet Union since the 1920s. Often the problems began with, or were complicated by, clashes between the Soviet Union's different ethnic groups.

In February 1988 the parliament in Nagorny Karabakh, an autonomous region of Azerbaijan, voted to return to the jurisdiction of Armenia (for earlier history see above, p. 94). This triggered demonstrations in Armenia and counter-demonstrations in Azerbaijan in which a number of Armenians were killed. The attention of the world's press was attracted, although the Soviet authorities at first forbade journalists to visit the area. Fate now took a hand. On 7 December 1988 Armenia was struck by a great earthquake, which killed nearly 30,000 people. The attention of the world was now irrevocably focused on the area. In January 1989 Nagorny-Karabakh was placed under the direct rule of Moscow but a virtual state of civil war now existed, which Moscow vainly strove to suppress. In January 1990 a demonstration in Baku, the Azerbaijan capital, called for the resignation of the communist government and its replacement by a Popular Front one. On 19 January Soviet troops moved in in earnest. Over 100 civilians, including children, died. But, as in East Germany, force could no longer intimidate the people. Azerbaijan declared itself independent in August 1991 and a Popular Front government took over in 1992.

In Georgia there were hostile demonstrations in November 1988 and in February 1989 during what were supposed to be celebrations of the anniversary of the incorporation of Georgia into the Soviet Union. In April 1989 Soviet troops fired on demonstrators in the capital, Tbilisi, and 21 died. This was followed by general strikes and protest meetings. Elections in 1990 brought the nationalists to power and they declared the treaties of 1921–2 by which Georgia had joined the Soviet Union to be invalid. Georgia formally declared itself independent in May 1991.

Determined efforts had been made to assimilate Moldavia, annexed under the terms of the Molotov–Ribbentrop Pact. A new language was invented, 'Moldavian', actually Romanian written in the Cyrillic script. It was therefore a considerable act of political defiance when in 1988–9 a literary weekly, *Literatur si arta*, began to publish in Latin script. The Moldavians changed the language laws and renamed the country 'Moldova' (its name as a Romanian province). But the Moldovans were not in any hurry to rejoin Romania, where Ceaușescu was still in power. Instead they too declared their independence in August 1991. (They also voted against reunion with Romania in a referendum in 1994.)

The story of Soviet Central Asia showed both similarities and contrasts with what had happened in the Caucasus. In Uzbekistan, as in Azerbaijan, unrest began with trouble between two ethnic groups. In June 1989 violence flared between the Uzbeks and the Meskhetian Turks, who had been deported to the region during the Second World War and were still living in shanty towns. Soviet forces were sent in to restore order but complete normality never returned and on 31 August 1991 the Uzbek parliament declared for independence. Tajikistan, which had lost important territory to Uzbekistan under Stalin, declared for independence in September 1991, as did Kyrgystan (Kirkizia). Turkmenistan (Turkmenia) declared its independence on 27 October 1991 but the communist Party, renamed the Democratic Party, remained in power. In Tajikistan a civil war developed between the communists and the Islamists. Trouble had come early to Kazakhstan. In February 1987 riots broke out when the Party Secretary, Dinmukhamed Kunaev, a Kazakh with a considerable network of local patronage, was replaced by an ethnic Russian. The riots were successfully suppressed by the police and the army and Kazakhstan was the last of the republics of the Soviet Union to declare its independence in December 1991.

Central Asia does not seem to have experienced either perestroika or glasnost as the rest of the Soviet Union did. Even in Soviet times the situation had remained an essentially colonial one with Russian bureaucracy imposed on older divisions and loyalties. When Russian control was removed, 'communist' parties survived, representing establishment groups and those in control more than any ideological force. The ideological forces came increasingly from resurgent Islam.

Central Asia was an outlying part, first of the tsarist and then of the Soviet empire, but even what had seemed part of the heartland of Russia, the Ukraine and White Russia (Belorussia) were affected by the changes. Ironically, dissent in the Ukraine began in Lvov, an old Polish university town, once part of the Austro–Hungarian empire, which had been annexed under the Molotov–Ribbentrop Pact and the annexation confirmed at Yalta in February 1945. The eastern Ukraine in contrast remained quiescent until a late stage. But in the course of 1989 a Popular Front for perestroika, which later became known as Rukh (the 'Movement') began to emerge. In September 1989 an attempt to celebrate the 50th anniversary of the annexation of Lvov turned sour. Thousands demonstrated and unfurled the blue and yellow Ukrainian flags. The same month Rukh held a conference in Kiev. In November the hard-line Party Secretary, Vladimir Shcherbitsky, was compelled to resign. Nevertheless, it was only the failed coup against Gorbachev which finally precipitated the Ukraine into a declaration of independence in August 1991, confirmed by a referendum in December. Even experienced observers were surprised that even the eastern Ukraine, with a large Russian minority, voted over 80 per cent in favour of independence. The result in the Crimea was even more surprising. The Crimea had been part of Russia from the time of Catherine the Great until Kruschev transferred it to the jurisdiction of the Ukraine in 1954, but even here the vote was, although only narrowly, for Ukrainian independence.

Belorussia was very slow to move. Perestroika seemed to be making little impact until in April 1991 economic stresses, and in particular a sharp rise in prices, triggered strikes. When the attempted coup came in August 1991, the Belorussian president, Nikolai Dementai, supported it. Its failure led to his resignation and a vote by the Belorussian parliament in favour of 'political and economic independence' although, in the view of some commentators, that was little more than a gesture.

What would replace the rapidly disintegrating Soviet empire? Nationalism should not have been a problem according to Marxist–Leninist theory. It was an atavistic response, which would disappear as genuine socialism replaced it. For many years Soviet politicians seem to have genuinely believed that they had dealt well with 'the nationalities question'. When he came to power in 1988 Gorbachev himself does not seem to have regarded nationalism as one of the most pressing problems. He had praised the Soviet Union as 'a qualitatively new social and international community . . . cemented by the same economic interests, ideology and political goals' (White, 1993, p. 172), although he had also acknowledged that some problems remained to be solved. In the light of the early disturbances in Kazakhstan and elsewhere, discussions began on the possibility of constitutional reform which would set a new framework for the state. The idea of a 'strong centre', combined with 'strong republics' (ibid., p. 174) became popular, although its precise meaning was unclear. In 1990 more concrete plans emerged for a 'union of sovereign states'. A referendum was held in March 1991 in which a large majority of those who voted supported the new proposals – but the Baltic states, along with Moldova, Georgia and Armenia, refused to take part.

A draft treaty was ready in July 1991 for a new 'Union of Soviet Sovereign Republics', which would have provided for common policies on defence, foreign affairs, transport and budgetary matters but which would have left all other legislation to the individual republics. Ironically, it was the proposal which led the hard-liners to mount the unsuccessful coup against Mikhail Gorbachev on 19 August. The coup was defeated by the president of Russia, Boris Yeltsin, and the determination of ordinary Muscovites. The attempted coup itself precipitated the declarations of independence by Latvia, Estonia, the Ukraine and other republics.

The draft union treaty was now dead and an attempt was made to replace it by the 'Commonwealth of Independent States', which would only maintain control over nuclear weapons and the currency and try to provide some economic co-ordination. In December 1991 the Upper House of the USSR Supreme Soviet voted for the dissolution of the Union of Soviet Socialist Republics. Gorbachev resigned as president and on 26 December the USSR formally ceased to exist.The successor states successfully sought membership of the United Nations and the new Russian Federation took the Soviet Union's seat on the Security Council.

The Commonwealth of Independent States continued a troubled existence. For Belarus and the Ukraine it served some useful purpose. Other states drifted in and out. It 1998 it included 12 of the former Soviet Republics – the Baltic states never had any interest in joining. The common currency collapsed in July 1993 and the central command of nuclear weapons was abolished the same month. Nevertheless, the CIS has provided a forum for discussing problems arising from the break up of the Soviet Union, including border questions, and opportunities for some degree of economic co-operation and co-ordination of defence policy – although the Ukraine and Moldova chose to remain outside the last.

The Russian Federation comprised three-quarters of the old USSR but its troubles were by no means over. Its members included 49 regions, 6 autonomous territories and 21 republics, as well as the cities of Moscow and St. Petersburg. Not all accepted this new status happily. The worst problems occurred in the republic of Chechnya, which refused to sign the Russian Federal Treaty in March 1992. Civil war began in December 1994. Chechnya was predominantly Muslim in religion and, in September 1997, introduced Sharia law. The Ukraine too was faced by a new independence movement in the Crimea, to which substantial numbers of Tatars (also Muslims), who had been exiled in 1944 for supposed German sympathies, had finally returned. The Soviet Union had been an integrated, as well as a command, economy and, as in Africa and the Indian sub-continent, adjustment to the new divisions seemed likely to be a long and painful process.

The Soviet Union, the one great European land empire, had broken up into its component parts almost more thoroughly than had the maritime empires. Its speed too had been breath-taking, accelerating even faster than the decolonization of Africa. So far as the satellites were concerned, Timothy Garton Ash had famously said in Prague in November 1989, 'In Poland it took ten years [to regain their independence], in Hungary ten months, in East Germany ten weeks: perhaps in Czechoslovakia it will take ten days.' (Ash, 1990, p. 78). The time scale had been comparable within the Soviet Union itself. Only four years elapsed between the first stirrings of discontent and the last republic's declaration of independence.

Conclusion

With the end of the Portuguese empire in 1975 the story of the rise and fall of the European maritime empires, which had lasted nearly five hundred years, came full circle. Only the two land-based empires, those of Russia and the United States, which had risen side by side with those of the maritime states of Western Europe, remained. That of Russia was to last another sixteen years. Russia and America were both to play their part in the collapse of the maritime empires.

For the American people the problem was a complex one. Decolonization was a cause to which, because of their own history, they felt a sentimental attachment. They saw their expansion over the North American continent as their 'manifest destiny', but the possession of overseas territories embarrassed them. They refused to retain possession of Cuba after the Spanish–American war in 1898. Nevertheless, by the mid-twentieth century they still had a scattering of overseas territories, Puerto Rico, the Virgin Islands, Guam, Wake and Midway Islands, American Samoa and Hawaii. Hawaii became a full state of the Union in 1959 but Puerto Rico turned down the chance to do so in 1998. The Philippine Islands, also captured from Spain in 1898, was the most obviously 'colonial' American possession. Only in 1946 did the Americans finally grant the Filipinos their independence, carefully transferring power to an oligarchy which they hoped would continue to support the Americans. It was a tactic which they were to favour in other sensitive areas as the Cold War developed, although not one which met with conspicuous success (Gifford and Louis, 1982, p. 2).

The Americans constituted themselves almost the patrons of decolonization at the end of the Second World War, but it was an enthusiasm which was tempered by the fear that the newly independent states might join the communist bloc. Their fears became most acute in Indochina. There was perhaps something in the old Whig adage that timely reform staved off revolution. In those countries where the decolonization process started early, the communists made little headway. There was a communist movement in British India, which received publicity – and possibly even encouragement – from the Meerut Conspiracy trials of 1929; but it was a feeble plant compared with the strength of the Congress Party. The French and the Portuguese, who resisted longer, left behind strong Marxist parties in many of their former colonies.

The relationship between nationalism and communism was a complicated one between the wars. After 1917 the Russians were, on the whole, too absorbed by the overwhelming economic and political problems of their own country to have many resources to spare for fostering revolutions in other people's empires. They made some, perhaps ritual, gestures towards recognizing colonial struggles as part of the proletarian movement, but there were ideological difficulties. Marx had taught that class struggle, not nationalism, was the way of the future. According to classical Marxist teachings, revolution would come from an urban proletariat, when capitalism and the ascendancy of the bourgeoisie had reached its final stage of decay. Marx had not envisaged the short-circuiting of this progression by peasant movements in countries which had not even undergone an industrial revolution. But neither the colonialists, nor the colonial nationalists, were for the most part concerned with the finer points of Marxist ideology. They were pragmatists. The colonial powers, in varying degrees, feared the Marxists. Their opponents, although they may have begun as nationalists rather than socialists, saw the tough and flexible organization of the communist 'cell' and some at least of them saw the advantages of attaching themselves to an international organization, particularly at a time when they still felt weak and isolated, confronting the apparently formidable might of a modern European state. Nevertheless, particularly in the later stages of the colonial revolution, they often derived their inspiration (and sometimes their practical help) from Cuba and China, rather than from Russia.

On the face of it, most western nations were still powerful at the end of the Second World War. The economic chaos of the late 1940s passed surprisingly quickly. In Britain 'austerity' was followed by the `affluent fifties'. Not many British dependencies, with admittedly the great exception of India, became independent during her period of greatest apparent weakness in the 1940s. Some historians have seen the relinquishment of the British empire as inevitable. Bernard Porter has suggested,

> From 1870 to 1970 the history of Britain was one of steady and almost unbroken decline. . . . The empire which she had accumulated towards the end of the [nineteenth] century, and then lost, was an incident in the course of that decline. It was acquired originally as a result of that decline, to stave it off. . . . And it was eventually surrendered as a final confirmation of that decline. (Porter, 1975, pp. 353–4)

In an interesting paper Paul Kennedy has questioned this judgement, suggesting that we may too easily have adopted Joseph Chamberlain's metaphor of the British empire even about the turn of the century as a 'weary Titan' and that we should rather be asking the question – why did it last so long? What function exactly was it serving? Why were so many people, not only in Britain but in the colonies, and even in the world at large, prepared to keep it going because it seemed to suit their interests to do so? (Kennedy, 1984, pp. 197–218). Other recent studies have also suggested that there are difficulties in accepting the view that about 1900, 'Britain was an ageing, defensive power struggling to fend off new challenges to her dominance' (Cain and Hopkins, 1993, vol. 1, p. 393). On the contrary they point to the pro-active, even dynamic, role of the City of London in the enlargement of empire.

It would be foolish to ignore the obvious. Europe's loss of its maritime empires was connected with the two wars, which broke out in the heart of the once dominant continent and quickly spread to become literally 'World Wars'. In recent years some political commentators such as Alan Clarke have begun to ask the hitherto unthinkable question: could Britain have saved her empire if she had declined to fight Germany in 1914 or 1939, or even made peace with Hitler in 1940? Questions of morality aside, it seems a dubious proposition. It would have left Germany in a totally dominant position on the continent of Europe. Would the Germans have been prepared to leave the British empire unmolested? Before 1914 the Germans had not disguised the fact that they had world ambitions. Hitler had found it politic to insist that he was only interested in *lebensraum* (living space) in the East and could happily coexist with the British empire but, by 1939, even the most credulous no longer believed Hitler's promises that each new claim was his 'final demand' and post-war research has revealed that the Germans were not so indifferent to the colonial question as they appeared (Crozier, 1988).

Once the decolonization movement started, it rapidly gained momentum until in the end it was almost as mad a scramble as the acquisition of colonies had been in the late nineteenth century. Why was this? Nearly as many explanations have been offered for this phenomenon as for the original colonization process and some of them link up interestingly with the rival explanations of the earlier movement. But the *Zeitgeist*, the spirit of the times, which is often included almost as an after thought in explanations of imperialism, is frequently invoked as a principal cause of decolonization. Social Darwinism and belief in evolution are generally presented as philosophical cloaks, justifying or explaining imperialist acquisitions made for hard-headed economic and political reasons. On the other hand, ideas of self-determination for all peoples, President Wilson's Fourteen Points, the Atlantic Charter, the Convenant of the League of Nations and the Charter of the United Nations are regarded as creating a climate of opinion which made the possession of colonial territories, contrary to the will of the inhabitants, seem intolerable. It is, of course, true that electorates in the metropolitan countries were wider by the mid-twentieth century than they had been a century earlier. Public opinion did count for more. Indian nationalists had discerned from a very early date that it was worth while appealing directly to the British electorate, bypassing the vested interests in Calcutta or London, although some like Tilak had been sceptical (Philips, 1962, pp. 161–3) and it had proved very difficult.

When asked for an explanation of the break-up of the Soviet empire in 1989 – or, more specifically, as to why the Soviet government did not intervene militarily to suppress the rebels as they had done in the 1950s – Timothy Garton Ash replied in three words, 'Gorbachev', 'Helsinki' and 'Tocqueville' (Ash, 1990, pp.140–2). Only the most hard-line of determinists would deny the role of individuals in the decolonization process – whether Mikhail Gorbachev, Charles de Gaulle or, on the other side, Mahatma Gandhi. Possibly the break-up of the empires would have come anyway but it would not have come in the way it did, and probably not at the time it did, but for the decisions and influence of individuals.

'Helsinki' was a reference to the 1975 Helsinki Agreement between 35 nations on European security and economics, which included promises on human rights. International law and with it standards of human rights had developed a great deal since the original tentative agreements, such as the Geneva Conventions of 1864 and 1906 and the Hague Conferences of 1899 and 1907, which had set up an international court of justice. The United Nations Universal Declaration of Human Rights of 1948 spoke uncompromisingly of equality before the law, rights of free election and the rights of all to take part in the government of their countries. In 1960 the General Assembly of the United Nations passed by 89 votes, with 9 abstentions, the Declaration on the Granting of Independence to Colonial Countries and Peoples. It began trenchantly, 'The subjection of peoples to alien subjugation, domination and exploitation constitutes a denial of fundamental human rights [and] is contrary to the Charter of the United Nations'. The wish of Russian and East European politicians to 'stand well' in the eyes of the world was a factor although, as Ash also points out, this was not entirely unconnected with the fear that hard currency aid might be withheld if they did not conform to the Helsinki Agreement.

'Tocqueville' was a reference to the French political scientist Alexis de Tocqueville's view that the decisive factor in a successful revolution was 'the ruling elite's loss of belief in its own right to rule'. This would seem to be true both of Gorbachev's Russia and of the western colonial nations. Morally Britain had conceded India's right to self-determination before 1947. Even those countries which, initially, defended their position by force, lost faith when that force proved ineffective or too expensive.

John Darwin (1991) in one of the best analyses of the causes of decolonization (although it is confined to the British case) considers the importance of changes in public opinion. After referring to Corelli Barnett's (1972) suggestion that it was the growth of 'moral squeamishness' that destroyed the empire and John Gallagher's (1982) belief that it was indifference, he examines the idea that it was connected with changing social forces in Britain itself (Darwin, 1991, pp.13–15). It has been proposed that the empire was always the concern mainly of the upper class and that the rise to power of the working (or middle) class might be expected to destroy it. This idea was most famously and ringingly advanced in A. J. P. Taylor's peroration at the end of his *English History, 1914–1945*: 'The British empire declined; the condition of the people improved. Few now sang "Land of Hope and Glory". Few even sang "England Arise". England had risen all the same.' Similar ideas were endorsed by John Strachey (1959), A. P. Thornton (1959; 1968) and R. Holland (1985). Darwin believes that popular support for the Suez adventure in 1956 and the Falklands war in 1982 demonstrates that the picture was not so simple and suggests that this can, at least partly, be explained by the fact that there were 'several' British empires, the colonies of settlement, India and the colonial empire mainly in Africa. They did not evoke the same public response and popular reaction was likely to be varied and sometimes unpredictable. In short, the abandonment of empire cannot be explained, at any rate in any simple way, by a seismic shift in public opinion.

Among intangible forces it is increasingly impossible to discount the role of religion and its hold on human minds. Even the atheist Joseph Stalin, when he wished to unite the Russian people to resist the Nazi invaders during the Second World War, suspended his persecution of the Orthodox Church and appealed, not to Marxist–Leninist doctrines, but to the concept of 'Holy Mother Russia', a twin appeal to nationalism and traditional religion.

In Poland the rebels rallied round the Roman Catholic Church, as they had traditionally done in their struggles with tsarist Russia. The visit of the pope in 1979 undoubtedly helped to trigger national consciousness. In East Germany too the independence movement began with the churches. This may, in part, be a simple reflection of the practical fact that people had comparative freedom of association in the churches. The role of the churches did not continue to be prominent in East Germany. Even in Poland, once freedom had been attained, the Poles showed themselves no more enthusiastic about the Church's hard-line on sexual matters, including contraception and abortion, than they had on the communist hard-line on the collectivization of agriculture.

Islam is also a continuous thread in the story. Even in the nineteenth century perceptive men, including the eccentric but well-informed Wilfrid Scawen Blunt (Blunt, 1907), saw the resurgence of Islam as a potent force for the future. Professors Robinson and Gallagher saw the partition of Africa as at least in part due to 'an involuntary reaction of Europe to the various proto-nationalisms of Islam' (*New Cambridge Modern History*, 1962, vol. XI, pp. 594–5). One such 'proto-nationalism' was undoubtedly the Mahdi's movement in the Sudan, which would today be recognized as an Islamic fundamentalist one.

The relationship between Islam and decolonization is not, however, a simple one. A sense of Islamic identity and a consequent unwillingness to accept French citizenship, if it meant abandoning that legal identity, undoubtedly helped to negate French plans in Algeria, when incorporation into metropolitan France was a possible alternative to independence for the 'assimilated'. Islam was a rallying call by the time the Algerian war was underway. But in India the Muslims, fearing the Hindu majority, co-operated with Britain, particularly during the Second World War. In most instances a considerable time has elapsed between the attainment of independence and attempts to set up an Islamic state with, for example, Sharia law, in former colonies.

Buddhism played some part in rousing resistance to the French in Indochina. The killing of a woman and eight children at a peaceful Buddhist celebration in Hué in May 1963 turned Buddhists against Diem's government. As part of the widespread protests, an elderly Buddhist monk committed suicide by burning himself to death in a Saigon street. 'A photograph of the grisly spectacle leaped off every front page in the world the next morning' (Karnow, 1983,

p. 281). But it was the secular, communist forces of Ho Chi Minh which finally defeated the Americans.

In India Tilak had played the card of traditional Hinduism against the British at the beginning of the twentieth century but Gandhi's position was a great deal more subtle. He appealed to the Indian masses as a recognizable 'holy man' but he did not hesitate to question the tenets of traditional Hinduism on matters such as 'Untouchability'. The first leader of independent India, Motilal Nehru, was determined to establish an impartial secular state. In India, as in parts of the Islamic world, it was the 1980s and 1990s which saw the rise of religious politics in the form of a Hindu nationalist party, the BJP.

If the role of religion in the decolonization process was sometimes ambiguous, its role in some quasi- or post-colonial situations, in Ireland, the Lebanon, or Bosnia, has sometimes been far from benevolent.

Not all modern explanations of decolonization place much weight on intangible forces. Some give short shrift to the suggestion that a more enlightened conscience in the metropolitan countries played a major part in decolonization. They look rather to changing material interests of the developed countries. Some fall into what has been called (Tomlinson, 1982, p. 60) 'the fancy footwork theory'. The British government, in particular, in adopting a more 'liberal' policy towards colonial nationalism between the wars was not preparing for the dissolution of the British empire but for its survival in an adapted form. 'The besetting sin of the policy makers was not galloping defeatism but, if anything, an excess of confidence in their ability, by a timely redeployment of the imperial factor,to outflank those elements in colonial nationalism which demanded a complete separation from Britain or the repudiation of her claims to political, economic or strategic privileges' (Darwin, 1980, p. 678). Such an explanation would, of course, fit very comfortably with the theories advanced by Professors Robinson and Gallagher in the 1950s and 1960s about the essential continuity of British imperial policy, which sometimes called for formal control over other parts of the world but was most typically best served by informal 'influence' (Robinson and Gallagher, 1953, pp. 1–15). Gallagher indeed approached this view himself when he said in his

Ford lectures in 1974, 'There was an increasingly good case for capitulating to the views of the age that imperialism was an obsolete method of projecting influence in the outside world' (Gallagher, 1982, p. 153). Darwin (1991, p. 5), however, cautions against too facile an acceptance of the attractive idea that a `redefinition of national interests' was `the motor of change'. There is, he points out, little evidence that redefinition of interests *preceded* the breakup of the imperial system. At times (ibid., pp. 45–7) economic crisis could actually lead to a temporary regalvanizing of the empire and an attempt to defend the sterling area. Britain's (successful) action in Malaysia in the late 1940s and early 1950s was directly connected with the importance of Malayan tin and rubber to the stability of sterling. At the same time it is undeniable that the empire/commonwealth was playing a declining part in the British economy. In 1950 it accounted for nearly half Britain's international trade; by 1970 that proportion had dropped to one quarter.

By the 1950s it had become clear that empire could be expensive both in monetary terms and, if you chose to defend it militarily, as the French and the Portuguese were to do, in terms of human resources and of political stability at home as well. Was it worth it? Almost certainly not, if you could leave behind a sufficiently stable political structure to provide a satisfactory trading partner; that after all, Robinson and Gallagher had argued, was what the Europeans had been seeking in the nineteenth century; they had only moved into formal political control when they could not find it. The growing nationalist movements seemed likely to provide such a political structure. They were usually headed by men educated and trained in western forms who, although they might not be liked by the traditionalists in their own societies, were quite acceptable to western politicians. This helps to explain the otherwise extraordinary revolution in British attitudes to Africa in the late 1950s and early 1960s when men such as Nkrumah and Kenyatta were released from gaol to head governments.

In the British case the first postwar decolonizations, mainly in Asia, were carried out by the Labour government of 1945–51. On the face of it this was to be expected. The Labour movement from the days of Keir Hardie and Ramsay Macdonald had been more sympathetic than the Conservatives to colonial aspirations, identifying them to some extent with the struggles of the British work-ing classes for their own form of self-determination. It was some-how appropriate that Clement Attlee, who had sat on the Simon Commission and protested about the inadequacy of the 1935 Gov-ernment of India Act, should pass the measure for Indian inde-pendence in 1947.

But, just as there had never been a clear-cut division between the political left and the political right about the desirability of acquiring an extended empire in the nineteenth century, so there was no clear division in their thinking about decolonization. The complexities are well analysed by David Goldsworthy (1971). Sometimes the attitudes taken were surprising. Winston Churchill lamented the impending independence of Burma in the passage quoted on p. 65, but it was the Labour deputy leader, Herbert Morrison, who said that giving Britain's African colonies inde-pendence would be 'like giving a child of ten a latch-key, a bank account and a shot-gun' (quoted in Cross, 1968, p. 262). Attlee himself regretted that Britain might be turning to Europe rather than to the Commonwealth. He said in the Commons in 1948 that he was 'disturbed by the suggestion . . . that we might somehow get closer to Europe than to our Commonwealth. The Common-wealth nations are our closest friends . . . we have to bear in mind that we are not solely a European Power but a member of a great Commonwealth and Empire' (quoted in Madgwick et al., 1982, p. 288). Some vocal opposition to decolonization came from the ex-treme right, such as the Suez Group, but it was in fact Conserva-tive administrations which, between 1951 and 1964, were responsible for the decolonization of practically the whole of Brit-ish Africa.

Two final points may be touched upon: the question of 'neo-colonialism', and the implications of decolonization for Marxist theory. It was a truism of English nineteenth-century textbooks that the British government intervened in India in the late eight-eenth century in order to check the excesses of the English East India Company. This aspect has often been forgotten since. Few European colonial governments were totally irresponsible. If they were not checked by their own consciences, or the forces of public opinion, they were restrained by the expectation that they would still be governing the colony for the foreseeable future. They had every interest in making sure that it remained reasonably prosperous and was not stripped of all its assets. Multinational companies have no such automatic check upon their operations. In some areas, at least, it would seem that neo-colonialism has proved worse than colonialism.

Ironically, the dissolution of the European empires caused more theoretical problems for Marxist historians than for others. When Lenin wrote his short book, *Imperialism: The Highest Stage of Capitalism* (in an earlier draft it was subtitled 'the last stage of capitalism) in 1916, it treated European imperialism almost as an apocalyptic sign of the coming of the millennium, the proletarian revolution which would overthrow the capitalist system. No one questioned then, or for another fifty years, that Lenin was using 'imperialism' in the sense then generally attributed to it, the conquest of the rest of the world by the European or western powers. Only when it became apparent that the empires were disappearing but that capitalism remained did the theoretical difficulties become apparent. The result was a major reassessment by Marxist (and some non-Marxist) historians of the role of imperialism in the Marxist framework of history. The most accessible discussions are in Kemp and Barratt Brown's contributions to Owen and Sutcliffe (1972, pp. 1–70) and one of the earliest, and still one of the best, the late Professor Eric Stokes's article in the Historical Journal (Stokes, 1969, pp. 285–301). 'Imperialism' has been reinterpreted in a highly technical manner to mean a certain form of the organization of capitalism.

The first phase of the 'liberation struggles' of the Third World is now virtually over. Scarcely any colonies, in the old sense, remain. It has, however, become painfully apparent, as Chief Awolowo predicted, that independence is not 'the Kingdom of God' (Awolowo, 1947, p. 30). The process of nation-building goes on, complicated both by internal political rivalries and by worldwide economic crises which, if they have caused distress in the developed world, have sometimes been catastrophic for the newly emergent nations of Asia and Africa.

It was nationalism, essentially a western concept (see above, p. 18), which proved the subject peoples' strongest ideological weapon against the colonizers. But it may be that nationalism itself is coming to be regarded as a barren concept (vehement feelings although it can still arouse). Multinational companies and the general concept of a global economy erode it from one side. From another there would seem to be a greater willingness to pool sovereignty for the common good. The creation of the European Union is an obvious example. The increasing tendency to believe that it is the United Nations' job to sort out problems and conflicts (however often it may have failed or attained only partial success) represents a sea-change from the 'Age of Nationalism' which so largely created the European empires and, in its colonial mirror-image, overthrew them.

Guide to Further Reading

The literature on decolonization is now vast and becoming vaster as the archives, particularly the British archives, open for the relevant period. The massive publication of 'British Documents on the End of Empire' got underway with the appearance of R. Hyam's *The Labour Government and the End of Empire* (HMSO) in 1992 and these will now join the equally massive *India: The Transfer of Power*, edited by N. Mansergh, 12 vols (HMSO, 1970–83). The following is intended only as a guide to some of the works available. Most of the books mentioned contain bibliographies, which give more detailed guidance.

Several general surveys of the European empires include interesting, although usually short, sections on decolonization. These include D. K. Fieldhouse, *The Colonial Empires: A Comparative Survey from the Eighteenth Century*, 2nd revd edn (Macmillan, 1982) and V. G. Kiernan, *European Empires from Conquest to Collapse, 1815–1960* (Fontana, 1982; an unfashionable but stimulating Marxist view). This is also true of some books on the British empire such as Bernard Porter, *The Lion's Share: A Short History of British Imperialism* (Longman, 1975: 3rd edn 1996) and T. O. Lloyd, *The British Empire, 1558–1983* (Short History of the Modern World) (Oxford University Press, 1984). Unlike earlier works a good recent study, D. Judd, *Empire: The British Imperial Experience from 1765 to the Present* (HarperCollins, 1996) deals at some length with decolonization. C. A. Bayly, *Atlas of the British Empire: A New Perspective on the British Empire from 1500 to the Present* (Macdonald, 1989) includes a good deal of analytical text as well as maps. Some classic works have been updated: for example, N. Mansergh, *The Commonwealth Experience*, vol. 2, *From British to Multiracial Commonwealth* (Weidenfeld and Nicolson, 1982), but on the Commonwealth see also W. D. McIntyre, *The Significance of the Commonwealth, 1965–1990* (Macmillan, 1995).

There are now rather more books which attempt to discuss decolonization across the board. These include H. Grimal (trans. S. de Vos),

Decolonization: The British, French, Dutch and Belgian Empires, 1919–1963 (Routledge and Kegan Paul, 1978); R. F. Holland, *European Decolonization, 1918–1981: An Introductory Survey* (Macmillan, 1985) and Franz Ansprenger, *The Dissolution of the Colonial Empires* (Routledge, 1989). D. Birmingham, *The Decolonization of Africa* (UCL Press, 1995) is a good introduction to that continent. John Keay's *Last Post: The End of Empire in the Far East* (J. Murray, 1997), which includes America and the Philippines, is lively and sometimes provocative.

The subject is so large that many of the most important volumes are collective works with papers on individual topics by leading specialists. Among these are P. Gifford and W. R. Louis (eds), *France and Britain in Africa: Imperial Rivalry and Colonial Rule* (Yale University Press, 1971), which takes the story up to about 1967, and the same editors' *The Transfer of Power in Africa: Decolonization, 1940–1960*, and *Decolonization and African Independence: The Transfer of Power, 1960–1980* (Yale University Press, 1982 and 1988); W. H. Morris-Jones and G. Fischer (eds), *Decolonization and After: The British and French Experience*, (Cass, 1980); and W. J. Mommsen and J. Osterhammel (eds), *Imperialism and After* (German Historical Institute, 1986). Dealing across the board with a particular area there are R. A. Oliver (general ed.), *History of East Africa*, esp. vol. 2, ed. V. Harlow and E. M. Chilver (Oxford University Press, 1965) and vol. 3, ed. D. A. Low and A. Smith (Oxford University Press, 1976) and J. Hargreaves, *The End of Colonial Rule in West Africa* (Macmillan, 1979), which incorporates his Historical Association pamphlet (1976) of the same title and other essays. Two comparative studies are M. Kahler, *Decolonization in Britain and France* (Princeton University Press, 1984) and J. Kent, *The Internationalization of Colonialism: Britain, France and Black Africa, 1939–1956* (Oxford University Press, 1992). John Hatch, *A History of Post-War Africa* (Andre Deutsch, 1965, written by a journalist with first-hand knowledge, remains a useful introduction.

Of particular interest in discussing the response of Africa to the West are: P. D. Curtin (ed.), *Africa and the West: Intellectual Responses to European Culture* (University of Wisconsin Press, 1972); R. W. July, *The Origins of Modern African Thought* (Faber & Faber, 1968); Thomas Hodgkin, *Nationalism in Colonial Africa* (Frederick Muller, 1956); and J. Ayo Langley's collection of documents with introduction, *Ideologies of Liberation in Black Africa, 1856–1970* (Rex Collings, 1979). The writings of various African nationalists, many of them autobiographical, also supply new insights. They include O. Awolowo, *Path to Nigerian Freedom* (Faber & Faber, 1947); K. Nkrumah, *Autobiography* (Nelson, 1957); and Joshua Nkomo, *The Story of my Life* (Methuen, 1984).

Many Indian nationalists also left personal accounts. Particularly central are: M. K. Gandhi, *An Autobiography: The Story of My Experiments with Truth* (Penguin, 1982) and J. Nehru, *Autobiography: Towards*

Freedom (John Lane, 1942). There are a number of good lives of the leading figures. Among them are Judith Brown, *Gandhi, Prisoner of Hope* (Yale University Press, 1989); Louis Fischer, *The Life of Mahatma Gandhi* (Granada, 1982); Michael Brecher, *Nehru: A Political Biography* (Oxford University Press, 1959); and S. Gopal, *Jawaharlal Nehru: A Biography*, 3 vols (Cape, 1975–84). There is an important revisionist study of Jinnah in Akbar S. Ahmed, *Jinnah, Pakistan and Islamic Identity* (Routledge, 1997).

The best general introduction to India is Judith Brown, *Modern India: the Origins of an Asian Democracy* (Oxford University Press, 1985). Other important books include Anil Seal, *The Emergence of Indian Nationalism: Competition and Collaboration in the Late Nineteenth Century* (Oxford University Press, 1968); R. J. Moore, *Liberalism and Indian Politics, 1872–1922* (Edward Arnold, 1966) and *Escape from Empire: The Attlee Government and the Indian Problem* (Clarendon Press, 1983); S. A.Wolpert, *Tilak and Gokhale: Revolution and Reform in the Making of Modern India* (University of California Press, 1962); and B. N. Pandey, *The Break-up of British India* (Macmillan, 1969). Invaluable is C. H. Philips's collection of documents, *The Evolution of India and Pakistan*, 1858–1947 (Oxford University Press, 1962).

The British was the largest empire and the most has been written about it. The best single book on the dissolution of the British empire is J. Darwin, *Britain and Decolonization: The Retreat from Empire in the Postwar World* (Macmillan, 1987). He has also written an excellent analysis of the various interpretations of that dissolution, *The End of the British Empire* (Blackwell Publishers, 1991). The demise of the empire is shrewdly considered by Colin Cross (a journalist with first-hand experience) in *The Fall of the British Empire, 1918–1968* (Hodder & Stoughton, 1968) and in G. Woodcock, *Who Killed the British Empire?* (Jonathan Cape, 1974). The third volume in James Morris's trilogy, *Farewell the Trumpets: an Imperial Retreat* (Penguin, 1979), is anecdotal but colourful. J. Gallagher (ed. Anil Seal), *The Decline, Revival and Fall of the British Empire* (Cambridge University Press, 1982) is a collection of papers, some previously unpublished, which illuminate various aspects of British imperial history.

A number of books examine the dissolution of the empire in the context of British domestic politics. Among them are P. S. Gupta, *Imperialism and the Labour Movement, 1914–1964* (Macmillan, 1975); David Goldsworthy, *Colonial Issues in British Politics, 1945–1961* (Oxford University Press, 1971); Stephen Howe, *Anticolonialism in British Politics: The Left and the End of Empire, 1918–1964* (Clarendon Press, 1993); and P. Murphy, *Party Politics and Decolonization: The Conservative Party and British Colonial Policy in Tropical Africa, 1951–1964* (Cambridge University Press, 1995). W. R. Louis, *Imperialism at Bay, 1941–1945: the United States and the Decolonization of the British Empire* (Clarendon

Press, 1977), discusses America's influence on the dissolution of the empire. Two books deal with the contribution of individuals, J. W. Cell, *Hailey: A Study in British Imperialism, 1872–1969*, (Cambridge University Press, 1992) and Clyde Sanger, *Malcolm Macdonald: Bringing an Empire to an End* (Liverpool University Press, 1995). A. N. Porter and A. J. Stockwell, *British Imperial Policy and Decolonization, 1938–1964*, 2 vols (Macmillan, 1987, 1989) is an important collection of documents with a substantial introduction. There are a number of studies of military aspects, among them C. J. Bartlett, *The Long Retreat: A Short History of British Defence Policy, 1945–1970* (Macmillan, 1972) and R. Neillands, *A Fighting Retreat: The British Empire, 1947–1997* (Coronet Books, 1996).

There is still a shortage of English material on the French empire, apart from Indochina, but there is P. Neres, *French-Speaking Africa: From Colonial Status to Independence* (Oxford University Press, 1962); V. Thompson and R. Adloff, *The Emerging States of French Equatorial Africa* (Oxford University Press, 1960); D. Bruce Marshall, *The French Colonial Myth and Constitution-Making in the Fourth Republic* (Yale University Press, 1973); and Paul C. Sorum, *Intellectuals and Decolonization in France* (University of North Carolina Press, 1977). A. Clayton, *The Wars of French Decolonization* (Longman, 1994) looks at a good deal more than the military aspects. The classic work on Algeria is still A. Horne, *A Savage War of Peace* (Macmillan, 1996). Vietnam has naturally attracted particular attention. Useful books include Ralph Smith, *Vietnam and the West* (Heinemann, 1968); George Herring, *America's Longest War: The United States and Vietnam, 1950–1975* (John Wiley, 1979); and S. Karnow, *Vietnam: A History, the First Complete Account of Vietnam at War* (WGBH Education Foundation, 1983).

Books which look at post-independence problems are now too numerous to be listed but two which look at the immediate aftermath are R. Harris, *Independence and After: Revolution in Underdeveloped Countries* (Oxford University Press, 1962) and A. H. M. Kirk-Greene, *Stand By Your Radios* (African Studies Centre, Cambridge, 1981), which is an analysis of military coups in Africa.

Three books not easily classified but important are M. Perham, *African Outline* (Oxford University Press, 1966) and *The Colonial Reckoning (Reith Lectures)* (Collins, 1962); and A. P. Thornton, *Imperialism in the Twentieth Century* (Macmillan, 1978).

Many works in the Penguin African Library are still useful, not least because they were written while events were in progress. Among them may be mentioned B. Davidson, *Which Way Africa? The Search for a New Society* (1964) and *In the Eye of the Storm: Angola's People* (1975); and Martin Lomey, *Rhodesia: White Racism and Imperial Response* (1975).

R. Owen and B. Sutcliffe (eds), *Studies in the Theory of Imperialism*

(Longman, 1972) is still a stimulating clash of Marxist and anti-Marxist ideas. Some important controversies are still conveniently approached by way of articles: John Darwin, 'Imperialism in Decline? Tendencies in British Imperial Policy between the Wars', *Historical Journal*, 23 (1980) 657–79; B. R. Tomlinson, `The Contraction of England: National Decline and the Loss of Empire', *Journal of Imperial and Commonwealth History*, XI (1982) 58-72; and P. Kennedy, 'Why did the British Empire Last so Long?' in P. Kennedy, *Strategy and Diplomacy, 1870–1945* (Fontana, 1984, pp. 197–218).

As with the break-up of the maritime empires, some of the best early accounts of the collapse of the Soviet empire came from journalists and other eye-witnesses. These include Timothy Garton Ash, *We the People: The Revolutions of '89 Witnessed in Warsaw, Budapest, Berlin and Prague* (Granta Books, 1990) and *The Polish Revolution: Solidarity* (Granta Books, 1991); Steve Crawshaw, *Goodbye to the USSR: The Collapse of Soviet Power* (Bloomsbury, 1992); David Keithly, *The Collapse of East German Communism: The Year the Wall Came Down, 1989* (Praeger, 1992); and David Remnick, *Lenin's Tomb: The Last Days of the Soviet Empire* (Viking, 1993), which won the Pulitzer Prize. All these contribute stimulating analysis as well as personal observations. Another book with inside information, which adopts a biographical approach, is Dmitri Volkogonov (ed. and trans. H. Shukman), *The Rise and Fall of the Soviet Empire: Political Leaders from Lenin to Gorbachev* (HarperCollins, 1998). Stephen White's *After Gorbachev* (Cambridge University Press, 1993) is a straightforward but thoughtful account, aimed at filling the gap between academic monographs and student textbooks. Martin McCauley has edited two multi-authored works, *The Soviet Union under Gorbachev* and *Gorbachev and Perestroika* (Macmillan, 1987 and 1990) which provide background analysis – see in particular Bohdan Nahaylo's chapters on 'Nationalism'. See also Bohdan Nahaylo and Victor Swoboda, *Soviet Disunion: A History of the Nationalities Problem in the USSR* (New York, Free Press, 1990), and Graham Smith (ed.), *The Nationalities Question in the Soviet Union* (Longman, 1990). For particular aspects see Abraham Brumberg (ed.) *Poland: Genesis of a Revolution* (Random House, 1983) and Allen Paul, *Katyn: The Untold Story of Stalin's Polish Massacre* (Scribner's, 1991.

References

Ash, Timothy Garton 1990: *We the People: the Revolutions of '89 Witnessed in Warsaw, Budapest, Berlin and Prague.* Granta Books.

Awolowo, Obafemi 1947: *Path to Nigerian Freedom.* Faber & Faber.

Barnett, C. 1972: *The Collapse of British Power.* Eyre Methuen.

Bemis, S. F. 1955: *A Diplomatic History of the United States.* Holt, Rinehart, Winston.

Bennett, G. 1962: *The Concept of Empire: Burke to Attlee, 1774–1947.* A. & C. Black.

Blunt, W. S. 1907: *Secret History of the English Occupation of Egypt.* Unwin.

Breuning, E. C. M. and Chamberlain, M. E. (ed. & trans.) 1998: *F. Fabri, Bedarf Deutschland der Colonien?* Mellen.

Brown, Dee 1972: *Bury My Heart at Wounded Knee.* Pan.

Cain, P. and Hopkins, A. G. 1993: *British Imperialism*, vol. 2, *Crisis and Deconstruction.* Longman.

Campbell, A. E. 1960: *Great Britain and the United States, 1895-1903.* Longman.

Chamberlain, M. E. 1974: *Britain and India: The Interaction of Two Peoples.* David and Charles.

Colebrook, T. E. 1884: *Life of Mountstuart Elphinstone*, 2 vols. Murray.

Conrad, Joseph 1973: *Heart of Darkness.* Penguin.

Crawshaw, Steve 1992: *Goodbye to the USSR: The Collapse of Soviet Power.* Bloomsbury.

Cross, Colin 1968: *The Fall of the British Empire, 1918–1968.* Hodder & Stoughton.

Crozier, A. J. 1988: *Appeasement and Germany's Last Bid for Colonies.* Macmillan.

Darwin, John 1980: 'Imperialism in Decline? Tendencies in Imperial Policy between the Wars.' *Historical Journal*, 23, 657–79.

Darwin, John 1987: *Britain and Decolonization: The Retreat from Empire in the Post-war World.* Macmillan.

Darwin, John 1991: *The End of the British Empire: The Historical Debate*. Blackwell Publishers.

Figueiredo, Antonio de 1975: *Portugal: Fifty Years of Dictatorship*. Penguin.

Fox, James 1982: *White Mischief*. Jonathan Cape.

Gallagher, John 1982: *The Decline, Revival and Fall of the British Empire*, ed. Anil Seal. Cambridge University Press.

Gardiner, A. G. 1923: *Life of Sir William Harcourt*, vol. 2. Constable.

Gifford, P. and Louis, W. R. (eds) 1971: *France and Britain in Africa: Imperial and Colonial Rule*. Yale University Press.

Gifford, P. and Louis, W. R. (eds) 1982: *The Transfer of Power in Africa: Decolonization, 1940–1960*. Yale University Press.

Goldsworthy, David 1971: *Colonial Issues in British Politics, 1945–1961*. Oxford University Press.

Grimal, Henri 1978: *Decolonization: The British, French, Dutch and Belgian Empires, 1919–1963*, trans. Stephan de Vos. Routledge & Kegan Paul.

Hailey, W. M. 1953: *Native Administration in the British African Territories*, 5 vols. Colonial Office. Reprinted, AMS Press, 1979.

Hargreaves, J. D. 1979: *The End of Colonial Rule in West Africa*. Macmillan.

Harlow, Vincent 1952: *The Founding of the Second British Empire*, vol. 2. Longman.

Harmsworth Universal Encyclopaedia, vol. 8, 1923. Amalgamated Press.

Hatch, John 1965: *A History of Post War Africa*. Andre Deutsch.

Herring, George C. 1979: *America's Longest War: The United States and Vietnam, 1950–1975*. John Wiley.

Hodgkin, Thomas 1956. *Nationalism in Colonial Africa*. Fredrick Muller.

Holland, R. F. 1985. *European Decolonization: An Introductory Survey*. Macmillan.

July, R. W. 1968: *The Origins of Modern African Thought*. Faber & Faber.

Karnow, S. 1983: *Vietnam: A History, the First Complete Account of Vietnam at War*. WGBH Educational Foundation.

Keith, A. B. 1961: *Speeches and Documents on the British Dominions, 1918–1931: From Self-Government to National Sovereignty*. Oxford University Press.

Keithly, David 1992: *The Collapse of East German Communism: The Year the Wall Came Down, 1989*. Praeger.

Kennedy, Paul 1984: *Strategy and Diplomacy, 1870–1945*. Fontana.

Lenin, V. I. 1917: *Imperialism: The highest stage of capitalism*.

Low, D. A. 1971: *Buganda in Modern History*. Weidenfeld & Nicolson.

Macdonald, J. Ramsay 1910: *The Awakening of India*. Hodder & Stoughton.

Madgwick, P. J., Steeds, D. and Williams, L. J. 1982: *Britain since 1945*. Hutchinson.

Majumdar, R. C. 1961: *An Advanced History of India*. Macmillan.

Mansergh, Nicholas 1958: *Survey of British Commonwealth Affairs, 1939–1952*. Oxford University Press.

Morel, E. D. 1906: *Red Rubber*. Fisher Unwin.

New Cambridge Modern History, vol X1, ed. F.H. Hinsley 1962: Cambridge University Press.

Nkrumah, K. 1957: *Autobiography*. Nelson.

Owen, R. and Sutcliffe, B. (eds) 1972: *Studies in the Theory of Imperialism*. Longman.

Parry, J. H. and Sherlock, P. 1971: *A Short History of the West Indies*. Macmillan.

Philips, C. H. 1962: *The Evolution of India and Pakistan, 1858–1947*. Oxford University Press.

Porter, Bernard 1975 (3rd edn 1996): *The Lion's Share: A Short History of British Imperialism*. Longman.

Roberts, S. H. 1963: *The History of French Colonial Policy,1870-1925*. Cass.

Robinson, R. and Gallagher, J. 1953: 'The Imperialism of Free Trade.' *Economic History Review*, 2nd series, vol. 6, 1–15.

Sarraut, A. 1923: *La Mise en valeur des colonies françaises*. Payot.

Seligman, E. R. A. (ed.) 1932: *Encyclopaedia of the Social Sciences*. Macmillan.

Sen, Surendra Nath 1957: *Eighteen fifty-seven*. Government of India.

Smith, Ralph 1968: *Vietnam and the West*. Heinemann.

Spear, P. 1965: *A History of India*, vol. 2. Penguin.

Stokes, E. 1959: *English Utilitarians and India*. Oxford University Press.

Stokes, E. 1969: 'Late Nineteenth-Century Expansion and the Attack on the Theory of Economic Imperialism: A Case of Mistaken Identity?' *Historical Journal*, 12, 285–301.

Strachey, John, 1959: *The End of Empire*. Gollancz.

Thornton, A. P. 1959: *The Imperial Idea and its Enemies*. Macmillan.

Thornton, A. P. 1968: *For the File on Empire*. Macmillan.

Tomlinson, B. R. 1982: 'The Contraction of England: National Decline and the Loss of Empire.' *Journal of Imperial and Commonwealth History*, XL, 58–72.

Van Alstyne, R. W. 1960: *The American Empire: Its Historical Pattern and Evolution*. Historical Association.

Van Alstyne, R. W. 1974: *The Rising American Empire*. Norton.

Waley, Arthur 1958: *The Opium War through Chinese Eyes*. Allen & Unwin.

White, Stephen 1993: *After Gorbachev*. Cambridge University Press.

Index